A Field Guide to
Skills of the Australian Bushman

A Field Guide to Skills of the Australian Bushman

written and illustrated by

Ron Edwards

The Rams Skull Press

First published 1996
Copyright © Ron Edwards
all rights reserved

Ron Edwards
THE RAMS SKULL PRESS
12 Fairyland Rd
Kuranda,
Qld 4872
Australia
Ph 070 937474
Fax 070 514484

ISBN 1 875 872 07 8

Wholly set up and printed in Australia

Table of Contents

INTRODUCTION

In 1975 I wrote *Bushcraft 1 - Australian Traditional Bush Crafts*. Following this and a series of articles that I did for the magazine *Australasian Post* I received letters from all over Australia describing various skills and ideas that I had missed in my book.

At the same time I was moving around north Queensland talking to farmers, bush people, and station hands and gradually coming to realise that there was indeed enough material around to fill another book.

This book was called *Bushcraft 2 - Skills of the Australian Bushman* and was intended as a companion volume to *Bushcraft 1*. The earlier book naturally contains the most basic crafts but I think that in many ways this one is the more interesting, mainly because of all the information I have been given by old bush people about skills that have now vanished. My collecting is continuing and I am always pleased to hear from people with additional information, corrections, or ideas.

This Field Guide tries to present in a small format all the best parts of *Bushcraft 2*, but of course being only half the size it cannot contain all the information that is in the larger book. I have had to leave out a chapter on how to build a simple rowing boat, a section on how to make a net and also a chapter on bush musical instruments. But I have tried to include in this book all the handy hints from the larger book.

Ron Edwards
12 Fairyland Road, Kuranda Queensland 4872

Camping Tips

Camping was all part of pioneering. The settler would first explore and having chosen an area would camp on it while he built his first shelter. In this way the skills he developed while camping in the bush gradually merged into the pattern that grew around a more settled life.

For instance fencing wire billy-holders originated around an open camp fire and then found their way to the open fireplaces in the settlers' homes where they evolved into well made wrought iron items.

Unfortunately as time went on a lot of these good ideas were forgotten, and it is the aim of these books to try and preserve them.

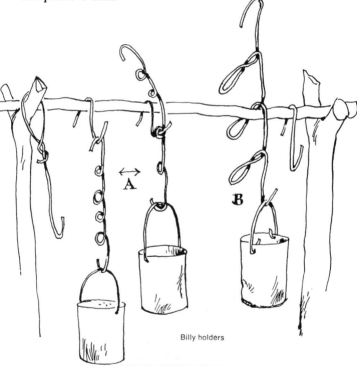

Billy holders

BILLY-HOLDERS

One problem with cooking over an open fire is how to arrange things so that while the tea billy boils the stew just simmers. The old-timers gave a lot of thought to this problem and came up with a number of answers.

One of the best and simplest was made from two pieces of fencing wire, shown as A in my sketch. One piece of wire was bent into a hook and the longer piece was twisted to form a number of loops with a hook at each end. With these loops the height of the billy could be easily adjusted.

The second sketch B shows another holder, made from a single length of wire twisted so that it had a number of built in hooks.

L. D. Appleton of Ayr, Queensland, said 'Many years ago I worked for the Queensland State Forestry and camped permanently. There were supposed to be four to a galley but we usually had eight in the gang. It was impracticable to put billies to the side of the fire so we used these adjustable hooks.'

Saucepan holder

SAUCEPAN HOOK

When W. H. Pearson of Yeoval, New South Wales, told me about this saucepan hook I was frankly sceptical. But he said that they were common sixty years ago and he had used them himself. I got hold of a piece of fencing wire and twisted one up and the result can be seen in the sketch.

I found that the fencing wire must be the thickest available and the saucepan should not be over-full. I was surprised at the way the pan was so firmly held in place, and with the wire at such a strange angle.

The pan is lifted on and off the fire by the hook, thus avoiding burnt fingers.

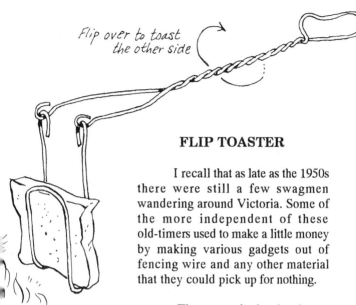

Flip over to toast the other side

FLIP TOASTER

I recall that as late as the 1950s there were still a few swagmen wandering around Victoria. Some of the more independent of these old-timers used to make a little money by making various gadgets out of fencing wire and any other material that they could pick up for nothing.

The toaster in the sketch cost me 20 cents and is the best of all toasters for a campfire. Everyone knows that feeling of frustration that comes while using a toaster with prongs when the half-done slice falls off into the fire.

The toast cannot fall off this toaster. It can be used while standing up or squatting down, against the fire or over the coals. By simply giving the handle a twist the bread flips over so that the other side can be done without having to touch the slice at all.

By the fire or over the coals

A toaster like this can be made with a pair of pliers, no other tools are needed. Two pieces of fencing wire are used, the handle is made from a piece 120 cm long and the toast holder from a piece 76 cm long.

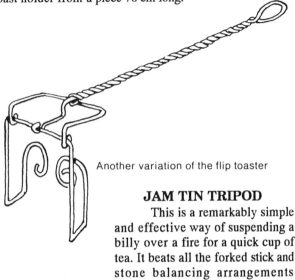

Another variation of the flip toaster

JAM TIN TRIPOD

This is a remarkably simple and effective way of suspending a billy over a fire for a quick cup of tea. It beats all the forked stick and stone balancing arrangements shown in camping books.

I have a tripod consisting of three pieces of steel rod and a length of chain, and this gets thrown in the truck with the camping gear. The jam-tin tripod is for use when travelling light.

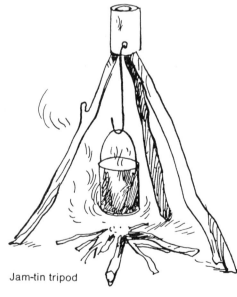

All that is needed is a jam tin and a length of fencing wire. Three sticks are pushed into the tin and the wire goes through a hole punched in its side. The wire loop can be adjusted to the height of the fire.

Darren Smith of Nunawading, Victoria, showed me this useful idea.

Jam-tin tripod

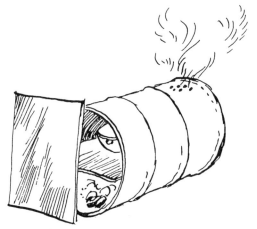

OIL DRUM OVEN

This must be the simplest of the various home-made ovens. When Reg Key was burr-cutting on Munga Bundie Station fifty years ago the camp boss knocked together an oven.

It was simply an open oil drum with a piece of flat iron jammed in as a shelf. Another piece of flat iron leaned against it as a door. Despite its simplicity Reg says that the cook used to do wonders with it: cooking cakes, pastries, and the fish that the men used to catch in their leisure time.

BUSH STOVES

In the open plains country where fuel was not plentiful, and strong winds frequently made cooking over an open fire impossible, the bushman would resort to a stove improvised from a small metal drum - usually a discarded 18-1itre oil drum.

In its simplest form a hole was cut in the side and a sheet of iron placed over the top to support whatever was being heated up.

A more efficient version had holes punched in the sides to take short lengths of steel rod on which the billy could be placed. This was better than the previous idea because the sides of the billy were now protected from the cooling effects of the wind, and also the use of steel rods rather than a solid sheet of metal allowed more heat to get to the sides and bottom of the billy.

As well as being a handy way to cook food and heat water the drum could also be used as a room heater in cold areas, and this next version was noted by Folklorist Warren Fahey in a pub at Wauchope, in New South Wales.

He said that the locals referred to it as a timber-tin.

The drum had been pierced with axe slits all over and had been mounted on rough legs. It was filled with glowing embers which had come from the hotel's hot-water system.

According to Warren the drum remained red hot for hours, without any topping up, and proved to be a most efficient room heater.

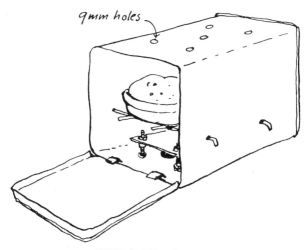

KERO TIN OVEN

The heavy wood stove was a rarity in remote bush camps which meant that the early settlers had to improvise if they wanted a baked dinner.

Clive Ditchburn said that this idea was popular in his boyhood days. It was one of the few ways in which the common primus stove could be used to bake things. Clive said 'My mother used it to bake scones over a primus and it took only a few minutes as no pre-heating was necessary. The tin got hot quickly and cooled off just as quickly. It was best used indoors out of the wind.'

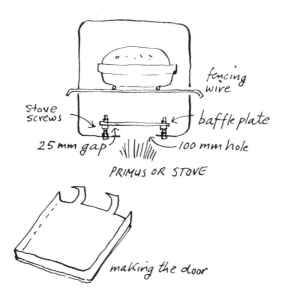

Two tins were needed for its construction, the bottom of one being used to make the door. The other had its top removed and was prepared as shown in the drawings. Ventilation holes were put in the top and a hole in the bottom to let in the heat. A baffle plate was put above the bottom hole to stop the food burning.

WIND DRYING FISH

In 1978 someone sent me a bundle of sketches and notes about bush ideas, but unfortunately did not include any name or address. I think that it may have been an old rabbiter because a few of the ideas were concerned with this business.

There was also this method of wind-drying fish. The fish is gutted as soon as it is caught and a stick is placed in it to expose the inside and then it is hung from the branch of a tree. A cloth goes round it during the day to keep flies away, but it is uncovered at night.

My correspondent said that a fish will keep for two or three days in this way. Of course, if there is plenty of coarse salt available in the camp, fish can be salted and dried and will keep for months, but this is a simple idea to keep a fish for a short time.

The idea will work whether the weather is hot or cold, but is not so good when the humidity is high. It needs dry moving air.

SALTING MEAT AND FISH

Fish are salted for longer storage with the same technique as that used for meat. A rough bench is made, usually with saplings for legs and a piece of old flat, or corrugated, iron for a top. The iron is fixed at a slight slope.

A generous amount of coarse salt is thrown over the fish or meat. Large slabs of meat are first cut into smaller pieces to allow the salt to penetrate.

The effect of the salt on the meat is to draw off all the liquids, and this is why the bench is set at an angle, allowing the juices to drain away from the meat. Curing is considered finished when the meat will no longer dissolve any salt and is bone dry.

The salted meat is stored by hanging it in a dry and airy place, it does not have to be covered as flies are no longer interested in it. I have only had the need to keep meat for a month or so but have been told that it will keep for well over a year if the weather is dry.

When cooking it is usual to boil it in a couple of changes of water to get rid of the excess salt. A slowly-simmered stew made from salted meat tastes nearly as good as fresh meat.

QUICK SALTING

This is a method that we used to use when going out for only a few days, in the days before I knew of the dangers of too much salt. Use steak sliced in the normal way, not in great thick slabs, and trim off all the fat. Get the frypan hot and at the same time cover the meat with as much salt as will stick to it. Cooking or table salt can be used.

Put the salted meat into the hot frypan and continually turn it, pressing down on it to expel the juices and simultaneously adding salt all the time. The idea is to sere and dry the outside without actually cooking the steak and at the same time give it a good coating of salt.

Depending on the weather and how well the job is done this meat will keep for a few days. To be on the safe side it is best to give it a light covering of salt and a couple of minutes in a dry hot frypan each day while in the camp.

SMOKING MEAT

We tried smoking meat a few years ago. The final flavour is governed by the type of timber used. During the centuries the overseas farmer has learned which of his local woods can be used for smoking and which are useless.

No one seems to have experimented with our north Queensland timbers so we had to work on trial and error. The result was a flavour completely different to anything I have ever tasted. It was pleasant enough but so unusual that we didn't feel like repeating the experiment.

Perhaps if smoking could be done above the cooking fire as part of the normal routine it would be a useful technique for the settler, but I found that the time taken to tend a special smoke house was out of proportion to the end result.

HEAT DRYING MEAT

This is the method used by the late Wally Brown when he was prospecting in north Queensland. Wally was over ninety at the time of telling me this so the method must be fairly safe.

He would make a container by cutting down a 200-1itre fuel drum to about 300 mm high and putting a fencing-wire handle on it. The lid was made by cutting down the other end of the drum to 75 mm. This would make a lid which was not airtight but close enough to prevent flies getting in.

He made a fireplace by putting two forked sticks in the ground with a crossbar between them on which hung the hooks for the various billies. The meat was trimmed of fat, put into the container, and hung over the fire.

The first time this was done the meat was constantly turned until it appeared to be quite dry. The lid was then put on and the container pushed to one end of the fireplace.

Each morning after breakfast was cooked he would pull the container across over the dying fire and give it about ten minutes of heat. In the evening he would do the same and in this way the meat was kept in a state of perfect dryness.

According to Wally "We would shoot a bloody goat on Prince of Wales Island, and we'd have that goat for about three weeks, and the last of that goat would still be lovely and sweet, it kept all the time. If you do that for ten minutes night and evening you can keep the meat forever."

KEEPING FOOD COOL

In the hot dry inland the settler always made some effort to stop the butter from turning into a liquid before it went on the bread and the milk from curdling before it was put into the tea. Refrigeration and the preservation of perishables was not aimed at, all that could be hoped for was a degree of coolness.

The Coolgardie safe was one of the most popular cooling ideas for many years. It was basically a wire frame over which was stretched some absorbent material that was kept moist. As the water evaporated the inside of the safe was kept cool.

I have a sketch of a standard type of Coolgardie safe in *Australian Traditional Bush Crafts* and there are a couple of variations in this book.

COLD HOLE

Ground coolers were a blessing to housewives in the days before refrigerators became available to country people.

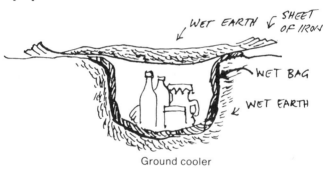

Ground cooler

The best position for them was near the water tank where the ground was often damp.

The example in my sketch came from Mrs M. Dickie of Swan Hill, Victoria, who said that with it bush people could keep food fresh for days.

A hole was dug in the ground and the soil was made as wet as possible. It was then lined with a wet bag and the food placed in it. A sheet of old iron on top and some wet soil on this and the cool hole was complete.

Mrs Dickie said 'It was colder than an ice chest; I know, because we used them.'

ANT STOPPER

Ben Constable of Yungaburra, Queensland, called this an Ant Mucker-upper. Like all bushman he fought a never-ending battle to stop ants getting to his food. I remember as a child that all our food cupboards used to have their legs standing in jam tins full of water. Ben's Mucker-upper was used with hanging meat safes.

A beer bottle had its bottom cut off by wrapping a string around it. This was soaked with metho according to Ben (we used to use kero), a match was applied, and when the bottle was guessed hot enough it was placed in a bucket of water. It would sometimes break off cleanly.

Another method of removing the bottom from a bottle is by putting a length of steel rod into the bottle and knocking the bottom out. It also works sometimes but is a little nerve racking.

A cork was placed in the bottle and through this was pushed a piece of wire. This hooked on to the ridge pole of the tent and held up the safe. The bottle was filled with water to make a moat against the ants.

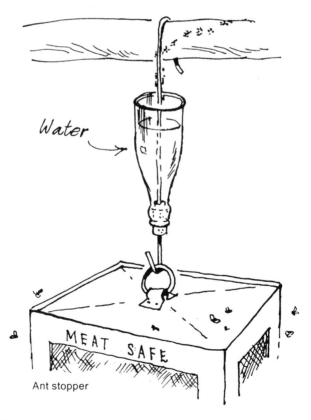

Water →

MEAT SAFE

Ant stopper

Bullocky's Meat Safe

This must have been the simplest meat safe yet devised. It took me only a couple of minutes to put one together to use this sketch, and only a few seconds to pull it apart afterwards. Of course the fact that we used horse feed sacks as floor mats in our house at that time made the job of getting the materials together a simple one.

Seventy year old Mr A. Millington of Renmark, South Australia, said that these safes were common along the Murray River in the early days and Mrs F. McPhillip of Corinda Beach, New South Wales, added that they were always used by bullock drivers.

A board was placed in a chaff bag to make the floor of the safe, the exact size was unimportant, I used one 500mm x 300mm. A couple of fencing-wire hooks were pushed through the bag and it was hung up in the shade and out of the reach of the dogs. The food was placed in it and the mouth of the bag tied with a piece of string.

The main purpose of this safe was to keep the food free from flies and insects. If hung in the shade and in a breeze it might also keep it reasonably cool.

There was always the risk of ants visiting the food by climbing down the wire hooks and seventy-year-old Allan Northey of Coolbellup, Western Australia, solved this problem by using half bottles filled with water as described on the previous page.

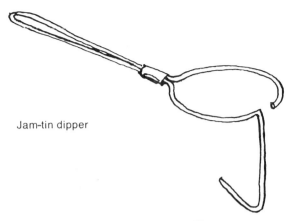

Jam-tin dipper

JAM-TIN DIPPER

Here is a simple dipper that was made from a jam tin and some fencing wire. It was described to me by W. Pearson of Yeoval, New South Wales. The fencing wire was bent to the shape shown in the sketch and a jam tin was pushed into place.

The wire was held together at the handle with a scrap of hoop iron hammered flat or a twist of tie wire. Bales and boxes used to arrive on stations bound together with a thin type of hoop iron which would be recycled for all sorts of purposes.

I have seen lattice work used to cover a verandah which had been woven entirely from the hoop iron that had been retrieved from bales.

As well as being used as a dipper the handle could also be used to hold a tin of soup or baked beans while heating it over the fire. The tin could be easily removed and replaced as desired.

KEEPING COOL

Ben Constable told me that when he was with a survey team on Cape York Peninsula in the 1950s they were billeted in tents. As summer approached the heat would become oppressive.

To help get the tents a little cooler they would hang their water bags inside and open the tents to whatever breeze was blowing. He said that it was surprising how the evaporating water helped drop the temperature.

SLUSH LAMP

J. Hetherington of Panania, New South Wales, told of a slush lamp used by an old silver-lead miner at Mt Robe, north of Broken Hill. It consisted of a jam tin which was three parts filled with sand and topped up with mutton fat.

The wick was made with a twig around which was wrapped a strip of fat-impregnated cloth. If clean fat was used the slush lamp was quite effective.

When I was a bachelor my mate and I relied at one time on a slush lamp and we used to use a bully beef tin full of dirty old fat with old cigarette butts for the wick. It gave a reasonable light but with a terrible stink and a lot of black smoke.

twig with cloth wrapping

mutton fat

sand

Slush lamp

Mrs Daisy Kelly of Ingham, Queensland, used to use slices of cow dung as a wick.

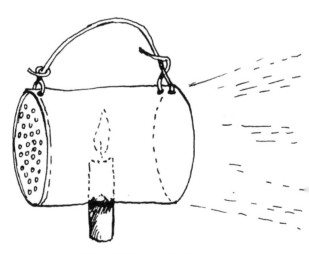

THE STORM KING

This grand name was given to a lantern made from a humble jam tin and a candle. The idea was passed on to me by Mr A. Whelan of Cardstone, Queensland, who recalled it from his boyhood in the Queensland mining town of Irvinebank.

The bottom of the tin had holes punched in it for ventilation and a hole in the side to hold the candle. A fencing-wire handle completed the Storm King. I was told that one great advantage of this lantern was that it did not throw light into the eyes of the person who was carrying it.

Where I live at present (1996) in Kuranda the power goes off on the average about once a week during the wet season and we have to rely on candles, kero lights and gas lamps, and I must admit that candles are about the weakest light that one could get.

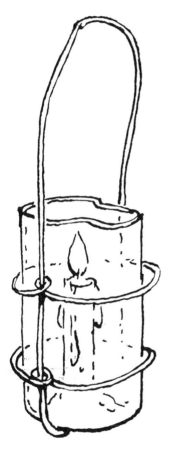

It takes at least four candles to get enough light to prepare a meal, so I would hate to have to rely on one in order to get somewhere at night, even with such a grand name as the Storm King. The oldtimers certainly did it the hard way.

BOTTLE LAMP

This simple style of bottle lamp was used in the north of Australia. It could be hung from the rafters or carried out of doors. It was simply made from a bottle with the neck removed, some wire and a candle.

FENCE BED

Mr S. C. Petlitt of Ipswich, Queensland, wrote about a bushman's bed in the days when post-and-rail fences were still common. Two sticks were buried in the ground and tied at the top. These held up one end of the bed poles and also the pole that held either the mosquito net or a waterproof sheet for wet weather.

Fence bed

The bed was made by threading a couple of sacks on to the long poles, an old bush trick that I have mentioned before.

THE SWAG

In inland Australia nearly all outside work is done during the dry season and this means that bushmen seldom have to worry about putting up a tent to protect them.

However, the inland can be bitterly cold during the night despite the high temperatures of the day. There are often numbing winds or heavy, soaking dews and the swag cover is essential to protect both the sleeper and his bedding.

During the daytime when moving camp the cover also contains and protects all the bushman's clothes and personal possessions. Everything he owns will either be on him or in this one big bundle. These swags are not meant to be carried by their owner as in the old days but are thrown into the back of the truck or strapped onto a packhorse.

The simplest swag cover is just a rectangle of canvas. When our children were small we used to use a piece of 4 metres square folded once, and this used to cover the four of us, below and above, in one big group.

There are many variations of swag covers, but they all have one aim in common and that is to keep out the weather. The set of sketches shows one used by N. McLennan of Auckland, New Zealand, when serving in the Western Desert during the war. He also used it in the New Zealand bush, which means that it must be shower proof.

It consists of a large rectangle of canvas with two flaps sewn on. The bushman throws his bedroll on to this upside down and then folds it as shown. He then turns the whole thing over.

In this way he has two layers of waterproof canvas under him as well as one of the flaps, allowing nowhere for the wind to enter. The other small flap, now on the top of the bed, can be pulled over the head if it rains.

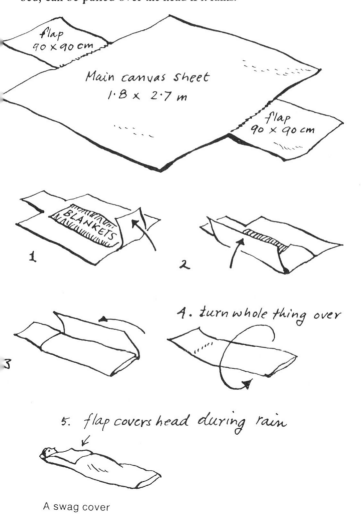

A swag cover

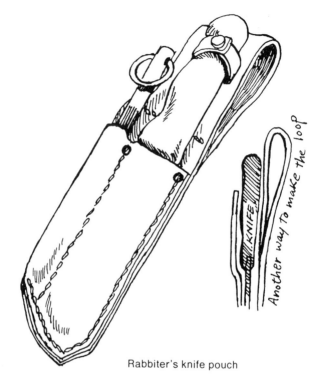

Rabbiter's knife pouch

RABBITER'S KNIFE POUCH

This idea is still being used by professional shooters and trappers who want their skinning knives to be razor sharp at all times.

The sheath is made wider than normal and a section is sewn to make a place to keep a sharpening steel. The press stud on the strap around the handle stops the knife from accidentally falling out.

Another form of sheath does away with this small strap. Instead the sheath covers most of the handle as shown in the small sketch.

Notice in the small sketch how the loop is formed from the sheath to slide on to the hunter's belt. In this case the leather is looped forward and finishes inside the pouch. This gives a smooth back to the sheath: it is no great advantage but it looks neater.

Gates and Fences

In *Bushcraft 1* I illustrated the most common gates and fences. Here are some of the more unusual ones, including some very clever ideas.

Curtain gate

TWO EXTRAORDINARY GATES

Well-known northern identity 'Bob Bloodwood' came across some odd gates in his travels and here are two examples. This is what he had to say of the Curtain Gate.

"On private station roads in central Queensland many years ago you sometimes came to a gateway where a number of slender sticks hung vertically, strung from a wire above.

"You crept forward in low gear parting the light sticks and they dragged over the vehicle. These gateways were not intended for the passage of good cars where paint might be scratched."

Gate for dim-witted cows

While this must have been a practical sort of gate Bob had reservations about the next one which I have christened 'a gate for dim-witted cows'. He described it as follows:

"There was a funny invention near Telmon on the Hughenden to Richmond road. You drove through an opening then first turned right, next turned left around the end of the netting and then turned right again.

"Cattle, horses, sheep, and pigs were supposed to look through the opening and seeing a fence ahead not know that they could walk round it by following the car tracks.

"How the councillors worked out that animals are less intelligent than the average car driver I'll never know."

A ROUGH OLD RAMP

I think that even the most stay-at-home city person will know what a cattle grid is. When people got tired of forever opening gates as they drove along the bush roads they replaced the gates with a hole in the ground covered over with lengths of logs. These days steel has replaced the logs.

One of the great disadvantages of a hole in the ground is that it tends to get filled up over a period and requires cleaning out. In parts of the country where there are dust storms cattle grids can fill up quickly.

On the blacksoil plains between Richmond and Hughenden on what was then the main road from Townsville to the Northern Territory some clever old bushman solved this problem by lifting the ramp above the ground. This was in the 1920s and a photograph appeared in the *North Queensland Register.*

Traffic ramp

As can be seen in my sketch the ramp was covered with lengths of log put far enough apart to stop stock climbing over it. It must have given a bone-rattling ride to the motorists of other days.

During 1977 in Bob Bloodwood's column in the *North Queensland Register* there were some heated exchanges between old-timers about the actual location of this ramp. It seems that it was on a road that once carried the traffic from Hughenden to Richmond but has since been relocated.

COUNTERBALANCED GATE

Mr S. C. Petlitt saw this gate on a sheep station near Surat, Queensland, many years ago. It is not hinged in the ordinary way but is balanced by a long cross arm at the top attached to the fence post with an iron spike.

Between the cross arm and the fence post is a small piece of hardwood that was kept greased for easier swinging. The gate hung from one side of the cross arm and a log was wired on to the other side to balance the weight of the gate.

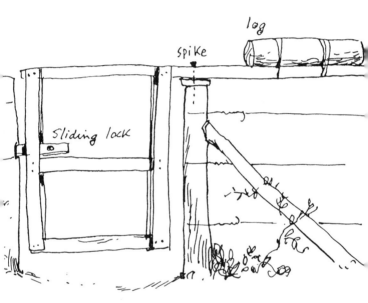

It seems that when the catch was undone the gate would gently swing open of its own accord, making it very handy for anyone who was carrying a pair of buckets. It only required a light push to close it again.

THE GRUNGE

The grunge was described to me by Rosina Noble of Arno Bay, South Australia. It was used in dairying areas where she was brought up and was intended for a person carrying a bucket to and from the milking shed.

A grunge

It was simply a gap in the fence with a centre post.
This post allowed the person carrying the bucket to get
through but prevented cows, and even calves, from escaping.

Stockproof gate

STOCKPROOF GATE

From P. Hession of Newcastle came the recollection
of a stockproof gate noticed in north Queensland. I saw the
same idea used at Lone Pine Sanctuary in Brisbane to stop
kangaroos getting into the wrong enclosure (but of course
the gate was much higher).

To operate it you pushed the gate away from you and walked into the space thus created. The gate was then swung to the other side and you walked out.

I have seen the same idea without a swinging gate, just a fixed panel. It works on the principle that a human can walk around a sharp angle but a cow or horse cannot twist enough to get around.

Garden gate

GARDEN GATE WITH BOTTLE HINGE

This gate demonstrates two old ideas which seem to have faded away. Mrs M. Jowett of Brooklyn, Victoria, said that her grandfather (born in 1848) used to hinge his gates in this way.

The first idea was the use of leather. In this age of plastic we forget how useful leather can be, and in this case a well-greased piece made the top hinge. It would last for years if kept greased and could be replaced in a minute.

The lower post of the gate was sharpened to a point and this sat in the indented bottom of the old type of vinegar bottles. Today a champagne bottle will do the same thing but looks as if you have a fancier life style.

FLYING FENCE POSTS

You have to watch out for flying fence posts if you ever visit Mirboo North in Victoria. Keith Jeffrey, a dairy farmer, told me that he moves fence posts by tying a length of fencing wire from a post at the top of a hill to a stout tree lower down.

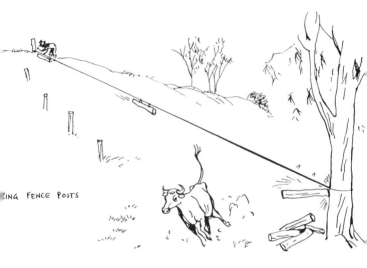

ING FENCE POSTS

The fence posts are attached to the wire with a couple of staples and speed off downwards -giving off a trail of white smoke, according to Keith. They hit the bottom tree with such a jar that the staples fly out and the posts drop to the ground.

This is a very simple idea, and yet it would save a large amount of work. Properly strained a length of wire could be used to carry goods for quite a distance.

I have seen a variation on this idea used to transport groceries from the top of a high bank, where the road was, down to the back of a house, but of course the box had a cord attached to it so that it could be slowed down before it hit the wall of the building.

STRAINING WIRE

Rob Prettejohn, past owner of Southedge Station told me about this method of tightening wire. It was used by the stockmen when they were out riding and did not have the proper tools for the job.

The wire was looped as shown in the small sketch and the other end passed through the loop. Then a forked stick was used, winding up the free end of wire and so tightening it.

Just as an experiment I have tried this method out with a length of wire tied to my car and another one to a tree. Using heavy fencing wire I found that I could pull the car out of the garage. This idea could also be used to slide heavy weights for short distances.

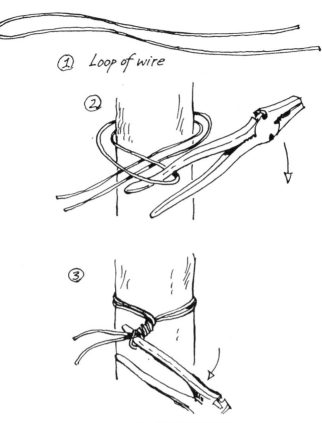

① Loop of wire

②

③

QUEENSLAND HITCH
(or COBB & CO. HITCH)

I was reminded of this hitch by Bill Thomson of Kinglake, Victoria. He called it a Queensland hitch, but in Queensland it is known as a Cobb & Co. hitch. It was illustrated in Bushcraft 1 but it is such a useful one that I have also included it here in more detail.

It is the most popular of all wire hitches and used for all sorts of jobs around the farm and camp. I have seen complete buildings put together without a nail, all the timbers being tied together with this hitch.

It requires no skill to tie; a length of fencing wire is doubled and then put around whatever is to be tied. A piece of metal, usually the handle of the fencing pliers or whatever is close at hand, is put into the loop and turned around until the hitch is tight.

One interesting aspect of the Cobb & Co hitch is that it can be used to apply pressure, as the winding takes place a surprising amount of leverage is exerted, so it is a useful hitch for pulling things together.

It is important when forming it to watch that both ends of the wire twist together, only in this way can they lock. When tied badly one pair of wires will just be wound around the others which remain straight, and if this happens the hitch will not grip.

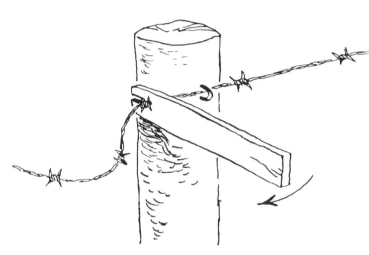

STRAINING BARBED WIRE

This old trick came from Bill Courtney of Sarina, Queensland. When straining barbed wire his father used to take a length of wooden paling and cut a narrow slit in one end with a saw. By slipping the slit in front of a barb and pulling back the wire could be strained while a staple was nailed in.

The Yard and Garden

There are a number of magazines available which cover the subject of this section in a warm and sensitive manner and I would suggest that anyone interested in self-sufficiency should subscribe to the ones that interest them. All I want to do here is jot down a few ideas that have been passed on to me and which I think will be of general interest.

Pig trough

HOLLOW LOG TROUGHS

Mrs Frieda Hintz of Toowoomba, Queensland, reminds me about the hollow log troughs still to be found on many old dairy farms. Hollow logs would be found when the settler cleared his land and it was a simple matter to split them and nail a piece of tin at each end to make a good, long-lasting, feed trough. I once found a beautiful native dugout canoe being used in this same way.

CHOOK'S CAFETERIA

Poultry can be a nuisance if they tie you down to the house to the extent that you cannot get away for a few days. These simple automatic food and drink dispensers help solve the problem.

The first, fig. A, came from Bill Courtney of Sarina, Queensland. It needs a couple of boards, two small tins, two bottles and some wire. The wire loops in the board support the bottles so that they don't quite touch the bottom of the tins.

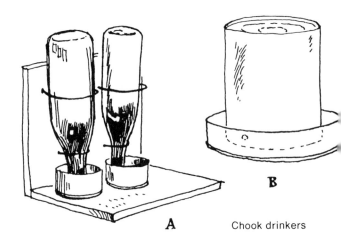

A   **B**

Chook drinkers

The bottles are upended and the water flows out to partly fill the tin. As the chooks drink the water level remains the same, and a glance at the bottle will show how much water is left. You may think that all the water would run out but it doesn't - another of nature's little wonders.

Sketch B shows a drinker that I made some years ago, it works on the same principle. A 4-litre paint tin has a small hole punched in it 15mm from the open end. It is then filled with water and upended into a slightly larger container made by cutting down another tin. The water will flow out to the depth of the small hole. A stone should be put on the top to discourage the chooks from sitting on it.

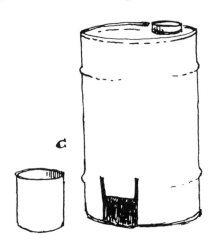

C

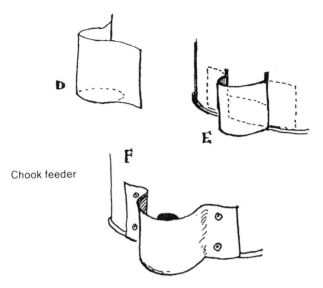

Chook feeder

Sketch C is a feeder. Any size drum can be used, we used a 4-1itre tin for a few bantams and a large oil drum for a larger number of chooks. If the drum has a removable lid so much the better, but the last one I made did not have one and the feed was poured through the top opening using a funnel.

The fowls feed from a small tin fitted at the base of the large tin. Two slits are cut in the large tin to the height of the small tin, as shown in my sketch, and a hole is made in between the slits half the height of the small tin. If the hole is made larger the chooks will be able to scatter the food everywhere as they feed.

Tool for cutting open oil drums

To cut open the drum use a very sharp cold chisel or a tomahawk. One of the best tools for cutting open drums was made for me by a friend years ago. It is simply a section of car spring 30 cm long, sharpened along one edge for a length of 10 cm. It is hit with a hammer and will remove a drum top better than most other tools.

The small tin is now opened up down the side with tin snips as shown in figure D. The opened-out ends are pushed through the slits and bent back inside the drum as shown in figure E.

If it is inconvenient to get inside the drum then the flap will have to be pop riveted on to the outside of it, in which case the upright slits in the drum are not needed, only the small hole for the feed to trickle through, see sketch F.

A DIBBER

Country people tend to keep everything, even after it has been broken. Here is an efficient dibber, for making holes in the garden in which to plant seedlings. It was knocked up in a couple of minutes from a broken spade handle.

SEED COLLECTOR

Today most people buy seed, but in the past it was usual to collect it. There were various methods of collecting seeds for different plants, and this was one method used for seeds such as clover. It was made with a jam tin opened at each end and with a bag tied on to collect the seed.

A V was cut in the tin and the seed head of the plant caught in the V. A quick pull allowed the seeds to be removed from the plant and they would fall into the bag. The idea came from George Leighfield of Glenroy, Victoria, and Ken Lomman of Naracoorte, South Australia.

For some years I have been collecting the seeds of our Chinese cabbage each season and keeping them in the frig until needed. I sow them using one of those condiment bottles that have a perforated lid.

Seed collector

LOTS OF POTATOES

Potatoes don't grow where I live, but Mrs Campbell of Northgate, Queensland, wrote to say that a big crop of them can be grown by planting them in the ground and then covering them with a large cask or box open at the top and bottom.

As they grow above the soil more dirt is added into the box and in this way an amazing number of spuds can be produced. Car tyres can be used in the same way.

JACOB'S LADDER

When the old-time north Queensland tin scratcher put down a shallow shaft he would sometimes construct what was known locally as a Jacob's ladder. This was a very simple ladder made by drilling holes through a stout length of timber, using a hand auger, and putting lengths of bloodwood in to make the rungs as shown in the sketch.

The ladder could be easily pulled out of the shaft when blasting was to take place. A couple of these ladders could be hooked together for greater length.

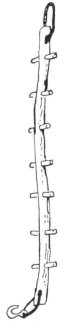

Jacob's ladder

GENTLE WATERING

Here are two ways to promote growth in young trees without wasting water. A bottle of water upended in the ground will slowly seep out. A 4-1itre paint tin with a small hole punched in the bottom has the advantage of being easier to top up and holds more water.

45

These ideas came from Ken Lomman of Naracoorte, South Australia and George Leighfield of Glenroy, Victoria. My son-in-law adds a little liquid fertiliser to the tin and feeds the plant at the same time as it is watered.

HOME-MADE SPANNER

Home-made spanner

This idea was sometimes used by farmers when they had no proper spanner. Any heavy, threaded rod could be used and a pair of square nuts screwed on to give the correct gap.

SELF STOPPING PUMP

L. Thomas of Emerald, Queensland, gave me this clever idea for a pump that will turn itself off when it has filled the water tank. He saw it on a friend's property at Clermont. When the tank is full of water it runs out of the overflow pipe and into a funnel and a hose.

The hose then runs the water into a billy can fixed to the pump in such a way that when it is full its weight pulls down on an arm that switches off the motor.

A similar principle was used by Joe Sedlbauer of Stratford, Queensland, to turn off a power hacksaw. He built a lever so that when the saw had finished its cut it would press against the switch and turn itself off.

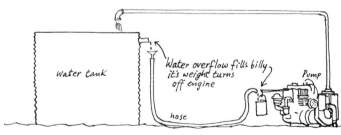

AUTOMATIC PUMP TURN OFF

SHORTING-OUT A MOTOR

L. Thomas passed on another method of automatic cut-off when pumping water, and this is probably the simplest. He would run an insulated wire from the spark plug of the pump motor and suspend its bare end at the height at which he wanted the tank filled. When the water reached this level it would contact the wire and cause a short-circuit which would turn off the motor.

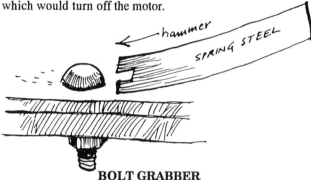

BOLT GRABBER

From Bill Courtney of Sarina, Queensland, came an idea for holding tight those annoying bolts that turn around when you are trying to undo them. He used a piece of spring steel 75 mm wide and 300 mm long. It has a notch cut into it the same width as the neck of the bolt. This is hammered in below the head of the bolt and holds it firm while the nut is removed.

SAND SIEVE

Up till recently this was still a common type of sieve in the bush used for both earth and sand. My trouble was that I could never find a bed frame that was not full of holes. The frame was simply propped up and the material to be sieved thrown at it with a shovel.

If sieving heavy material some fencing wire is laced across the springs to stop them sagging. Tim Chorley from Cuckoo Flat near Galston, NSW, told me about it.

TANK GAUGE

From Mr Pearson of Holland Park, Queensland, came an idea for a tank gauge that could be modified to suit any type of water tank. In 1976 he was working on a cattle station on the Condamine River and one of his jobs was to keep an eye on the level of water in the tanks.

On many stations the water tanks are up on high stumps and he got tired of climbing up to peer in and check the levels. This gauge was made by running a cotton reel between two pieces of timber. The cotton reel had a cord from it which went through a couple of pulleys and to a bottle which floated on the water.

The bottle had some sand in it so that it just floated. As the water level went down the bottle also dropped and pulled the cotton reel up between the sticks so that the level could be checked at a glance.

We use an even more simple variant of this idea, some fishing line is attached to the bottle and a small piece of scrap metal hangs from the end of the line outside the tank to act as a marker.

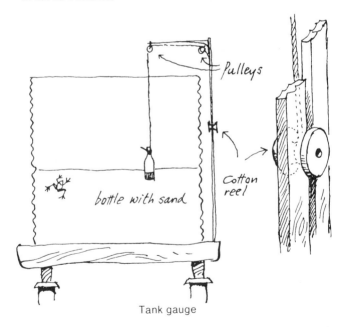

Tank gauge

Simple Building
STOCK CAMP ARCHITECTURE

The sketch was made on a station to the west of Chillagoe, Queensland, and is typical of the buildings commonly found around stock camps and outstations in north Australia. These buildings are characterised by wide roofs that come within a metre of the ground to provide the maximum protection from the fierce monsoon rains and still allow the greatest air circulation in the hot, tropic conditions.

They employ the simplest forms of construction, the frame being made of bush timber held together with fencing wire over which is laid a corrugated iron roof. The ends are often partly filled in with iron at the top to stop rain blowing in. Sometimes the roof is of double thickness, separated by lengths of saplings to provide extra insulation against the heat.

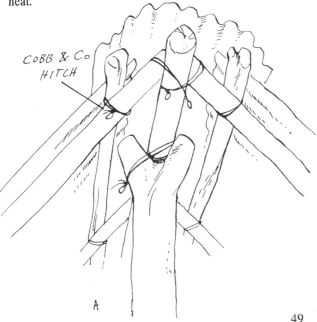

COBB & Co HITCH

A

The only tools needed to build this type of camp are an axe, a file or fencing pliers (to cut the wire and tie the knots in it), a hammer, and perhaps an auger bit if any of the logs need to be drilled.

All parts of the framework are tied together with fencing wire using the ever-popular Cobb & Co. hitch. The wire is doubled and wrapped around the object to be tied, and then the end of the file or the handle of the pliers is put into the loop as shown and twisted around while the left hand holds the loose ends of the wire.

When sufficient tension has been achieved the file is removed and the hitch is complete. The amount of pressure applied is surprisingly great and it is an easy matter to break the wire if care is not used.

The next sketches show details of the two buildings which comprise Prices Creek Outstation in the Queensland Gulf Country. Sketch A, previous page, shows the ridge pole being supported by a forked log set into the ground. This is the strongest and simplest method. Note how all the timbers are tied to one another with Cobb & Co. hitches.

The lower ends of the roof were supported by forked posts of around one metre high as in (B). The roof was then nailed down on to this frame. In some old camps the roof is not nailed but is held down with more timbers which are wired to those below.

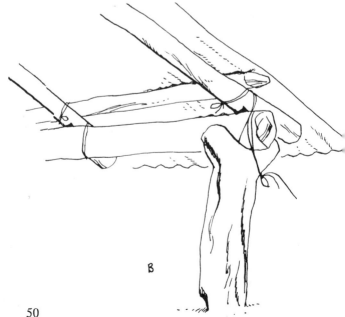

B

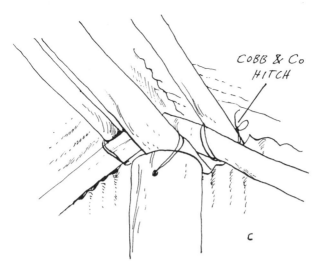

COBB & Co
HITCH

c

The larger building was the most recent, and the ridge was supported by a plain sawn upright pole. In this case a hole had to be drilled to take the wires to tie down the ridge pole as shown above.

TILT-UP WALLS

I have been told that the idea of tilt-up walls originated in New Zealand. This may not be so, but the idea is certainly used there in the construction of farm buildings. Tilt-up walls are cheap to make and are very strong.

Briefly the idea is that first the cement floor is prepared. This is then covered with plastic, or even paper, and a section of wall is prepared on the floor. When it has cured it is then lifted into position.

Some years ago the New Zealand Cement Association produced a free booklet on this method and I obtained a copy through the Concrete Association of Australia, which had branches in all capital cities. They also had a booklet showing how the idea has been used in Australia to produce huge wall slabs for factories.

A few years ago I modified the idea and used it to construct a building measuring 12 metres x 5 metres. Because I had no machinery to lift the slabs I made them much smaller than usual - 900mcm wide and the height of the wall.

A wooden frame was set up with a plastic sheet underneath it. Holes were drilled through the wood at what would be the top of the wall and bolts were put into the holes to be set into the cement.

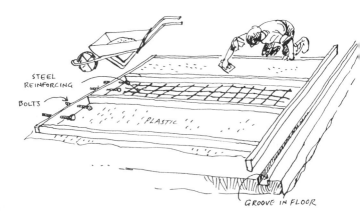

STEEL REINFORCING

BOLTS

PLASTIC

GROOVE IN FLOOR

Plenty of steel reinforcing was put into each section and then we used a cement hand mixer to make up each batch consisting of three parts of gravel, two of sand, and one of cement.

When finished this was covered with plastic and kept moist for a week to cure. The wooden frames were removed before this time. The panels were 75 mm thick, and although this does not sound much it took the combined effort of four of us to lift each of them into place.

They slipped into a groove in the cement floor and were propped up until finally locked into position. The original piece of timber frame with the holes in it dropped over the bolts to hold the wall in line, and the pieces of frame that divided the panels were also put back between them.

A wider plank was then bolted on each side as shown in the sketch. This building was completed in 1969 and has required no maintenance since then. The method of connecting each panel with its neighbour could be improved, but the rest of the idea seems to be very good.

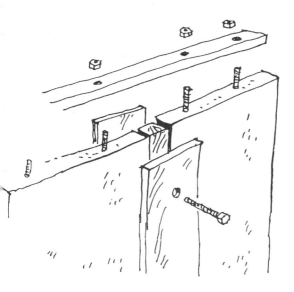

HURDLES FOR WATTLE AND DAUB WALLS

Early engravings show that the British introduced the art of hurdle making in Australia. Hurdles were in fact a form of prefabricated fence, and the shepherds would put a number of them together to make an enclosure for their sheep at nights.

With the acceptance of open range grazing the practice slowly faded away, doubtless helped by the fact that there were not so many suitable timbers in this country for hurdle making. However, when there were flexible sticks available hurdles were made with the aid of the log shown in the sketch.

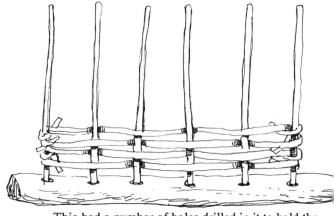

This had a number of holes drilled in it to hold the upright sticks for the hurdle. Flexible saplings, often split down the centre, were then woven in and out as shown until a section was completed.

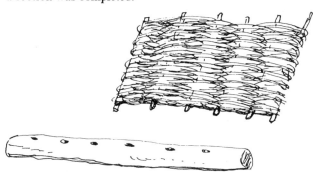

These same sections could also be used in the making of wattle-and-daub huts, the hurdles being attached to the upright posts where they made a good foundation for the applied mud.

SELF-LOCKING JOINT

A cabinet maker showed me this self-locking joint which was in use in the old days but has now almost been forgotten. It joins together the top wall plate, the stud, and the ceiling joist without using any bolts or nails. Once the rafters have been put in place along the top plate the joint is permanently locked in place.

Figure 1 shows the three pieces apart. Figure 2 shows the top plate sitting in position. When the ceiling joist is dropped over the others (figure 3) the joint is locked.

This method is only useful where large timbers are being used, it would be impractical with the small timbers used in modern buildings.

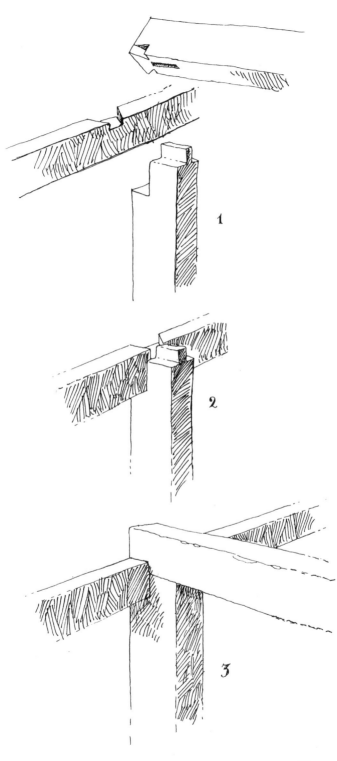

Kero Box Chest Of Drawers

The rectangular kero tin was a familiar sight to our pioneers. Kerosene was the most common fuel for lighting and it came in large tins. When sent to the country the tins were packed in pairs in wooden boxes.

Both the tins and the boxes were used by bush people for all sorts of things. Mrs Lola O'Brien of Gordonvale, Queensland, gave me a description of a chest of drawers made from them as illustrated.

The wooden boxes were tacked one on top of the other to make the framework. The tins had one side cut out of them and were placed back to act as the drawers. The sharp edges were bent over to avoid cut fingers.

BUSH TABLE

A common way of constructing small tables and stools is shown on the next page. The top of the table is a plank split as wide as possible, and the legs are simply lengths of saplings, in this case the bark was not even removed.

The top of each leg is shaped to form a shoulder so that the leg will not slip right through, and usually a wooden wedge is hammered in to make a tight fit once the legs are in place.

SMALL TABLE

This small table was made by Kym Dungey for the cottage he built at Koah, Queensland. The top is a single log split and opened out, while the legs are sections of smaller logs.

BUSH CHAIR

The sketch for this chair was taken from a photograph of a prospector's camp at Kalgoorlie, around 1892. It is a bush version of what I call a 'Yongala' chair, a type of deck chair that was common on ships around the turn of the century but is no longer found today.

(The *Yongala* was a coastal steamer that went down with all hands in a cyclone between Mackay and Townsville in March 1911. A deck chair that was washed off it is illustrated in *Bushcraft 1*.)

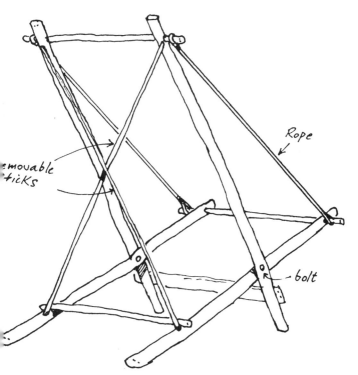

Its unusual feature was the way it was supported by a pair of stout cords that went from the front of the seat to the top of the back rest. This version had in addition a pair of light crossed sticks at the back, not to support the chair, as they were too light for this, but to stop it from moving sideways.

The material for the seat would have been easily obtained from the variety of bags that were used for wheat, sugar and stock feed in the old days. Jute and hessian bags were plentiful and were used for all sorts of purposes, such as curtains, or forming the base of a bed. When filled with straw or feathers they would also serve as a mattress. And of course swagmen used them to carry their belongings across the country.

The old photograph was not clear enough to see how the various timbers were attached. The small crossed sticks that went from the back of the back rest to the back of the seat supports may have been dowelled into place or they may have been simply held there with wire.

In either case they would have been attached in such a way that they could be removed easily, to allow the whole chair to fold up for easy transporting.

INDIAN CHAIR

I first saw this type of chair in use in a house near
Cairns in 1959. I don't know where the idea originated but
in later years I have heard it called an Indian chair and been
told that the American Indians used it in their tepees.

It is certainly simple to make, two ropes supporting
a stick and some material thrown over the stick. The sketch
is of a neighbour relaxing. It can be made more comfortable
by throwing some pillows on the floor. The one that I first
saw used an old car seat.

The car seat had been put on the floor and the material draped over it. When anyone sat on the chair their own weight kept the back firm as long as they were sitting on both layers of the material. It was also easy to adjust the angle of the back, it was just a question of where you sat on the material.

FOLD-UP STOOL

I sketched this stool at John William's home, Kuranda, Queensland in 1978. The seat was of strong leather with small pockets sewn in to hold the legs. The legs were of saplings held together with a short strap passing through wire loops hammered into the wood.

I have made similar stools using a Turk's Head (see the section on knots) to hold the legs together instead of wire loops. The whole stool will then slip apart in seconds when travelling.

These days it is also possible to buy special bolts with three legs which have been designed specially for making this type of chair.

Nails

Nails were always prized in the bush in the old days and people would laboriously pull apart packing cases or anything else that contained them. Even when I was a child it was still common for bush people to straighten out any nails that they could salvage and use them once again.

Fencing wire was a very popular resource because it was always available, and while bolts and long nails were expensive in the bush, and had to be ordered from the town, a shed or stockyard could be fastened together with wire and would be stronger than one that was nailed.

The settler also used the wire for any number of little things, toasters, toast racks, billy hooks, and so on, some of which are illustrated in other parts of this book.

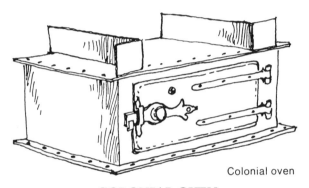

Colonial oven

COLONIAL OVEN

The Colonial Oven differed from the ordinary wood stove in two important ways. Firstly, because it consisted of only the oven section, it was considerably lighter than a full stove and so could be transported into remote bush areas where a heavy stove could not have been taken.

Secondly, it was a quarter of the cost. In 1911 a Colonial Oven was 12 shillings compared with 48 shillings for a full wood stove. Mrs Anne Porter, born in 1897, of Junee, New South Wales, cooked on one many years ago, at a time when her rent was 5 shillings a week.

The oven was bricked in the way that I have shown in the sketch on the next page, but using house bricks rather than rocks. Spaces were left for two fireplaces, one below the oven and one above it.

Home-made Colonial Oven

Mrs J. S. Price of Campsie, New South Wales, sent me a sketch of a home-made oven used by her grandparents around the turn of the century. A used metal drum took the place of the manufactured oven section with a piece of flat iron inside the drum to act as a shelf. The rest of the construction was of rock and iron as shown.

Mrs Price observed, "Many Christmas and birthday cakes were baked in an oven like this, besides scrub turkeys and roasts of beef".

EGG SLICE

Mrs Frieda Hintz of Toowoomba, Queensland, remembered many old do-it-yourself ideas, including an egg slice made from a piece of tin and some fencing wire. It could be made with skill and solder, or just knocked together quickly as shown here. In this version four holes were punched into the tin with a nail and the fencing wire threaded through them.

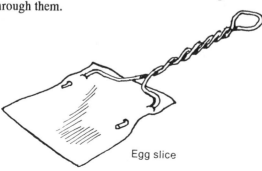

Egg slice

Kero Tin Washing-up Dish

Here is yet another example of the uses to which the kerosene tin could be put. On the next page there is a dust pan made from a kerosene tin, and in other volumes of this series there are yet more things made with both kero tins and the boxes in which they were packed. They were a highly prized item and I don't think that any were ever thrown away, there was always one more thing that could be made from them.

They were even cut open and flattened out to make the walls of miner's huts, and in the dry inland the metal would last for many years.

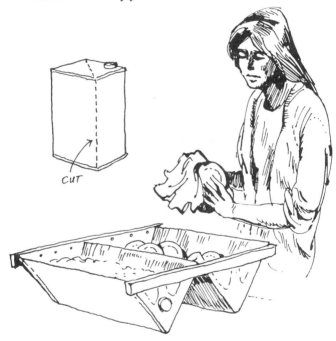

Kero tin washing dish

This washing-up dish was a favourite in the bush. An 18-1itre kero tin was cut as shown in my sketch and then folded out to form a double washing-up dish. A piece of wood or a strip of tin made it firm. One half would be used to hold the hot water and the other part acted as a draining dish, or would be filled with clean water to rinse the dishes.

The cut edges were usually turned over and hammered flat so that they would not cut fingers.

KERO TIN DUSTPAN

Mrs B. Geeson of Taylors Beach, Queensland recalled a handy dustpan made by cutting a kero tin on an angle and nailing a section to a length of broom handle.

The broom was an equally homemade affair using any sort of suitable material tied to a short handle.

WAGGA RUGS

The Wagga rug was common among farm families earlier this century and was born of economic necessity. When bush people could not afford blankets they made do by using the sacks that came into their hands, wheat bags, corn sacks, sugar bags and so on. These would be washed first to clean and soften them.

When clean the sacks were opened up and sewn into the shape needed for a blanket. Then any available material that could be found was sewn on to one side, squares cut from old clothes would do, but old scraps of blanket were even better.

This made a useful blanket 'warm as toast' as one informant said, and a good makeshift when the farmer could not afford to buy blankets for his family.

Bottle lamp

Home-made Kero Light

Mrs J. S. Price of Campsie, New South Wales, recalled a home-made lamp used by her grandparents in Queensland when she stayed with them around the turn of the century. Any wide-mouthed bottle could be used, and was filled with kerosene. The cork had a slit in it just big enough to take the piece of cloth that acted as the wick. To prevent the cork from charring, a lid from a syrup tin was also slit and placed above the cork. She said that "These lights were used by my grandparents and would not go out in the wind if used outside, which was what they were meant for".

Fishing Light

Years ago when we used to go spearing fish at night I made up a traditional fishing light which also used kerosene. A piece of scrap pipe made the kero container and also acted as the handle. Rags were jammed into this as a wick.

A large milk tin was cut away to provide both a reflector for the light and to prevent it shining in the fisherman's eyes.

With these lamps we would wander around on the tidal flats looking for fish sitting on the shallow bottom.

Fishing lamp

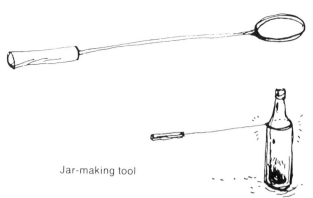

Jar-making tool

CUTTING BOTTLES

There are several methods of cutting bottles. Graham Mitchell of Cooranbong, New South Wales, tells of seeing his grandmother use the tool shown in the sketch. She cut the bottles down to use as preserving jars.

The round, iron ring was made so that when it was put over the neck of a bottle it stopped just at the place where the taper straightened out. The ring was made red hot and then placed on the bottle. After a few seconds it was removed and the bottle placed in a bucket of water 'top first'. He added that the top always broke away cleanly.

Tim Chorley of Fiddletown via Galston, New South Wales, had a different method. He said that he would fill a bottle with oil (usually old sump oil) to the level at which the break was required and would then insert the red hot handle of a branding iron into the bottle with the end sitting in the oil. According to Tim the bottle would break at the level of the oil.

A PIPE REAMER

Tim Chorley told me also of a pipe reamer (for tobacco not water pipes) made by fitting a short section of an old keyhole saw into a home-made handle. He said that it worked very well.

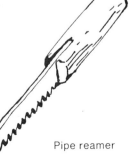

Pipe reamer

MOUSE SUICIDE

Mrs Joan Preston of Rozelle, New South Wales, recalled that during a mouse plague fifty years ago her father used this efficient mouse catcher. A piece of burnt cheese was put into the neck of a greasy bottle. The mice lost their footing on the bottle and fell into a bucket of water.

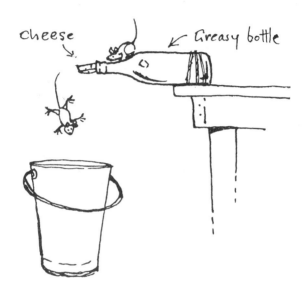

A GRUESOME MOUSE TRAP

Leonard Redfern of 'Strathlea' near South Wangaratta, Victoria, told me of a mouse trap guaranteed to spread pieces of mouse all over the room. He said that they had a plague of mice getting into the chicken feed and other stuff around the farm and that he didn't have enough ordinary mouse traps to keep them under control.

All Victorian farms have a few rabbit traps around the place so he devised a method of using these. The trap was set as lightly as possible and the cheese suspended above it by a piece of string, out of reach of the mice.

The frustrated mouse, unable to reach the cheese would try and jump up and catch it, and his descending weight would be enough to set off the trap with the results mentioned above.

Duck trap

A DUCK TRAP

Judging by the amount of advice I have received it seems that the Victorian's stock answer to catching anything is to put a container out and hope something falls into it.

Malcolm Fields of Kangaroo Flat, Victoria, told me of an old-time Tumble Trap used for wild duck. An ordinary 4-1itre paint tin is tied to a pole which is hammered into the bed of the lake with the rim of the tin just above the water.

Breadcrumbs are put in the bottom of the tin as bait. The theory is that when the simple-minded duck reaches down for the crumbs he will overbalance and fall head-first into the rim where he will be jammed.

Malcolm said that he has been told that this trap works but had not actually seen it in action. "But," he concluded "If a mouse is silly enough to fall into a drum then I would give this a fair chance of success."

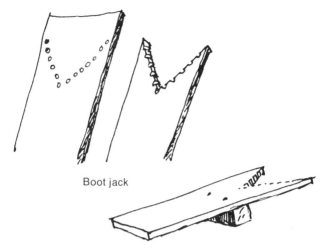

Boot jack

GUM-BOOT PULLER

Gum boots are praised by dairy farmers when they are working in wet, muddy yards, and later cursed when they are trying to pull them off. Tim Chorley uses an improved version of a very old idea.

By drilling a number of holes in a V and then sawing the shape out an edge is produced that will get a grip on the muddiest of boots.

WHITEWASH BRUSH

In the old days it was a simple matter to construct a rough broom by tying a bundle of twigs on to a stick. Sometimes even the handle was omitted.

I recall many years ago seeing Aboriginal women at Delta Downs Station in the Gulf Country using bundles of twigs as brooms. Bending double every morning it was their duty to sweep the bare earth around the main homestead for a distance of fifty or a hundred metres.

This had two purposes, the obvious one being that it made the place look neat. The second one was that the tracks of any person approaching the house were plainly visible and could be readily identified by the Aboriginal stockmen.

The whitewash brush in my sketch is a much more sophisticated tool than a bunch of twigs, but belongs to the same family. It was given to me many years ago and I don't know who made it.

Whitewash brush

Its handle was made from a piece of plank 260 x 120 x 13 mm. This had been roughly shaped as shown in the smaller sketch. The hair for the brush may have been cut from an old broom though being 150 mm long it would have to be an industrial one as it is much longer than that found in a household broom. The material was not hair but some natural plant fibre, perhaps a fine millet.

This had been gathered into two bundles and tied to the handle with copper wire. The notches at the bottom of the handle were put there to stop the wire from slipping off.

Two simple food coolers

TWO FOOD COOLERS

The old-time food cooler was not intended to preserve food like our modern refrigerators. Food was only kept in it for a short time and its main use was to keep drinks cool and the butter firm.

Mrs E. Hill of Lake Cargelligo, New South Wales, used two types of coolers over the years. Butter used to be packed in plywood boxes about 35 cm square and one of these would be sunk into damp ground on the shady side of the water tank. This would only work if the ground was kept constantly damp by a slow leak from the tap.

The other sort was made by opening the side of a kero tin and putting a smaller tin inside, then filling the gap with dirt. This dirt was kept damp and the food placed in the inner tin with a lid over the whole lot. This was kept in the shade and Mrs Hill said "It was surprising what coolness was held in this".

A QUICK COOL BEER

This is an old fisherman's tip, I have not tried it but Ben Constable said that it was very effective. If you want to cool down a couple of tins of beer and there is not enough ice left to do it then sprinkle a good amount of salt on what ice there is. This will cause the ice to melt much faster, but it will also chill the cans more effectively than would otherwise be possible.

Home-made Food Coolers

Before the days of refrigerators bush people kept their food cool by using the evaporation of water. When I was a lad we used a Coolgardie safe and this did the job quite well. It was made of a simple wire framework covered in towelling, like the one in my sketch but without the pyramid top.

Instead it had a tin tray on the top and my job was to keep this filled with water. Pieces of towelling hung in the water and the water crept up this towelling and slowly soaked down the sides, arriving at another tin tray at the bottom where it finally dripped into a bucket. The water in the bucket was then poured once more into the top tray.

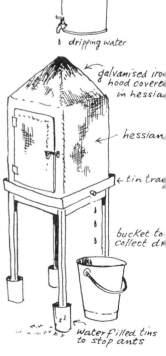

dripping water

galvanised iron hood covered in hessian

hessian

tin tray

bucket to collect dr

water filled tins to stop ants

Coolgardie safe with hood

The Coolgardie safe in my sketch is a variation that does not need a little boy to keep it going. It was described to me by Carl Bailey who had one like it in Merredin, Western Australia, in 1915.

Instead of a tray on the top there was a pyramid made from iron covered in hessian. Water constantly dripped on this and so soaked down the sides of the safe. The settlers used to make their own safes using fencing wire, bush timber, and hessian bags.

Mrs J. Hill of Toorak, Victoria, wrote to tell me that her grandfather Francis Benness worked on the goldfields at Kalgoorlie and Coolgardie, and was credited with the invention of the Coolgardie safe.

ROOM COOLER

Mrs Evelyn Coleman of Frankston, Victoria described an effective adaptation of the cooling principle used in the Coolgardie safe. It was during a terrible heat wave that caused the deaths of a number of people in the Melbourne area.

The atmosphere had become almost unbearable when Evelyn thought of the cooling effect of the old Coolgardie safe. Taking some flannelette sheets she soaked them in water and hung them over all the doors and windows, wherever the fiery north wind was blowing into the house.

She said "There was a miraculous change. Within ten minutes the house became pleasantly cool and the family restored again. The sheets needed to be soaked three times during the afternoon, but the day passed more pleasantly for us".

WEAVING SUN BLINDS

Charles Beresford of Malanda, Queensland, gave me details of this simple weaving method. Using bamboo and string he wove sun blinds for his whole house and verandah in less than a day.

Two rows of sticks are set into the ground. The back row is around 60 cm high and 150 mm apart and the front row is 30 cm high and 150 mm apart. These rows are placed with enough distance between them to allow for the depth of blind to be woven.

A piece of string is now tied between each of the front and back sticks. A second piece of string is then tied to each of the back sticks and these strings are 60 cm longer than the first strings. The longer strings are then tied to a long pole.

One worker then lifts this long pole up and down, and as he does so another person places a stick of bamboo (or any sort of suitable thin stick, or even a handful of dried rushes) in between the two strings. As the first worker raises and lowers the long pole the bamboo is caught between it.

Charles Beresford found that best results were obtained by having two people sitting on the ground packing in the rods tightly, one person slipping the rods into position and the fourth person raising and lowering the long pole.

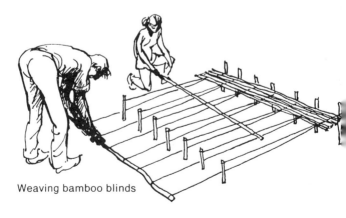

Weaving bamboo blinds

TOYS

TIPCAT

Who can remember the game of tipcat? It probably has a lot of different names and more rules than we used when I was at school in Victoria. We took a piece of wood about 40 mm long and pointed each end as shown in the sketch.

A circle was marked on the ground as a goal, and the idea was to get the tipcat into the circle in two strokes. First we put the stick under the cat and flicked it forward. Next we hit one of the ends with our stick, causing it to fly into the air.

In another version the cat had flat surfaces cut into it and each was marked with a number. The number that showed on the top indicated the number of strokes a player could take.

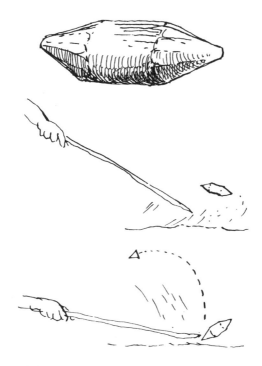

DOODLEBUCK (or DOODLEMBUCK)

Judging by the number of letters I have had on the subject, the doodlebuck was a well known toy along the east coast of Australia forty years ago. Although there were slight variations in design, certain things were basic.

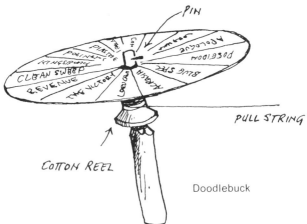

PIN

PULL STRING

COTTON REEL

Doodlebuck

It seems to have emerged each year at Melbourne Cup time. The names of the runners were written on a circle of card and this sat on a stick, as I have shown, or on a piece of wire and was spun. When it stopped, the name opposite the pin on the stick was the winner.

There was a jingle to go with the game 'Who'll have a go on my doodlebuck! Two and your own one back'. It seems that cherry stones or 'bobs' were the standard betting units.

STEAMROLLERS

In the 1960s all the kids in our area made steamrollers by filling powdered milk tins with sand and threading a wire through them. They would drag them around by the hour.

Sometimes they would link up three or four tins to make a road train.

BUSH BILLIARDS

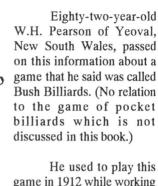

Eighty-two-year-old W.H. Pearson of Yeoval, New South Wales, passed on this information about a game that he said was called Bush Billiards. (No relation to the game of pocket billiards which is not discussed in this book.)

He used to play this game in 1912 while working at a timber camp in the Weddin Mountains. A line was drawn on the ground behind which the player stood. A circle of about 500mm diameter was marked out 6 metres away.

Five tins were placed in this circle as shown. They were inverted and holes punched in the bottom of each, from one to five holes.

The players nominated a number between 6 and 12. The player had three sticks around 70 cm long and with these he then tried to knock over three tins whose holes added up to the nominated number.

Mr Pearson added: "It wasn't real easy. We used to play it by the light of the waste timber fire at night. It was popular at one time in bush camps and shearing sheds".

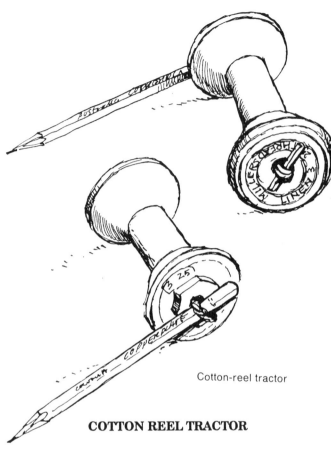

Cotton-reel tractor

COTTON REEL TRACTOR

This rubber-band-propelled toy has become rare due to the change in design of cotton reels. I was reminded of it by Mario Russo of Holloway Beach, Queensland, who said 'Plastic-age kids will have to miss out on this toy which was the focus of many a "Mine will climb steeper hills than Yours" challenge'.

It was simple to make, requiring a cotton reel, a pencil, a matchstick, and a strong rubber band. Better quality models also had a washer between the pencil and the cotton reel. This could be cut from leather or a tap washer, but the best ones were shaped from a slice of candle.

The rubber band had to be strong (bike tube was a favourite) and the pencil was wound around until the rubber would take no more. Placed on the ground the tractor would rumble away by itself.

Cotton car

COTTON CAR

Chris Longhurst of Lyons, A.C.T., sent me a sketch of another cotton-reel toy. This was a car made by joining two cotton reels together with a piece of fencing wire. It could be made in a minute and was almost unbreakable.

Chris says 'A more simple toy could not be imagined, but when I had one of these cars I was the envy of all the other kids'.

TIN CANOES

Mrs B. Geeson of Taylors Beach, Queensland told me the "old time inventions we had as children up in the sugar country of north Queensland". I was interested to discover that the tin canoes that kids used to make many years ago were the same as the ones that my son and his friends made decades later.

Construction was as simple as possible. An old piece of corrugated iron was roughly flattened out and folded around a piece of stick that formed the bow and another short length of board that made the stern. The lack of any form of caulking plus the usual number of holes in old sheets of iron meant that the sailor spent as much time bailing as rowing.

JAM-TIN STILTS

Children can get a great deal of fun out of the most simple toys. I must thank Miss H. Jamieson for reminding me about this idea. I remember my own kids tottering around the house on these stilts.

Any sort of jam tin can be used, getting high off the ground is not important. The tin is inverted and holes punched near the bottom. A loop of string goes through the holes. The kid stands on the tin and holds it to his feet with the string.

As Miss Jamieson remarks "Who said there are no cheap toys any more!"

PLAITER'S CLAMP

Nothing could be simpler than this clamp, it is merely a log or plank leaning against some vertical surface. The work is placed between the leaning pole and the upright and is held in place by the weight of the craftsman.

This clamp was sometimes used for rough bush plaiting with greenhide which would not be marked by the jamming effect of the leaning pole. It was more often used to hold the edge of a fresh skin when it was being scraped clean.

I thought this a great idea when I first saw it, but now find that a hook is a much better thing to hold a whip when plaiting it.

SEWING WITHOUT NEEDLES

The old-time shoemaker would twist a hog's bristle into the end of his waxed thread instead of a needle. He sewed the same way as when he used needles, first pushing a hole in the leather with his awl.

Tim Chorley of Galston, New South Wales, sent me an example of stitching done in an up-to-date version of this method. Having to repair a bridle in a hurry and not being able to find any needles he applied a spot of quick-setting glue to each end of the thread and formed it into a point before it dried.

Then he made the holes in the leather with his awl and found that the pointed threads worked quite well.

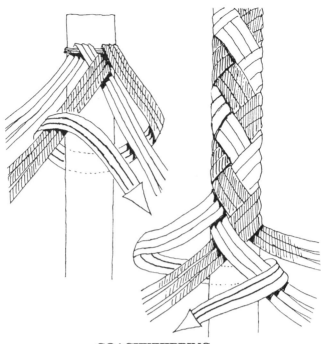

COACHWHIPPING

Once the beginner starts to work with more than eight strands plaiting in the round can become difficult because it can be hard to control a large number of strands with a limited number of fingers.

The most practical method of handling a large number of strands is known as coachwhipping. This is always done around some sort of central core, be it the leather belly of a whip or the handrail of a boat. It is also found on the handles of whips used by the drivers of carriages or coaches, and the name probably came from this.

The sketch on the left shows the beginning of coachwhipping using twelve strands. The *Ashley Book of Knots* suggests this as a neat method of beginning. The strands are divided into four groups, and the plaiting is exactly the same as for four single strands.

The two steps shown here are all that is needed to do this plait, they are repeated all the way down the job.

Using this method one simply divides the strands into the required number and then treats each group of strands as if it were a single strand. For instance, a sixteen-strand job would be handled by dividing the strands into eight groups of two and then using an eight plait.

However, you will probably find that the twelve plait shown here is quite enough to handle and would not recommend a beginner to attempt any more.

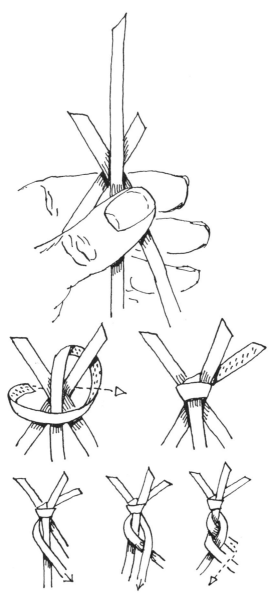

A PLAITED HATBAND
(Three strand)

I am indebted to Monty Salt, an Aboriginal stockman of Normanton, Queensland, for details of the hatband shown in the sketch. It is a flat three plait made from 3 mm kangaroo lace and is an easy project for the beginner.

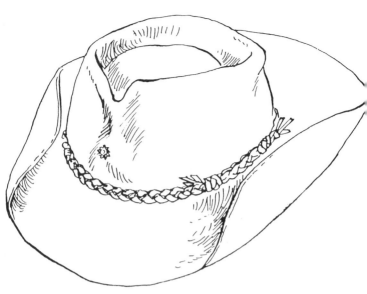

This was Monty Salt's hat.

Making the Band

Select three lengths of lace each about a 900mm long, this would suit the average adult when plaited and allow enough for some overlap. Hold the three pieces of lace as shown in the first sketch and tie the knot as shown.

I think that everyone knows how to do a simple three plait, but just in case I have shown how it starts. In order to hold the band firmly while plaiting is being done you can put it in a vice, or jam it in a cupboard door or close a drawer on it.

The plaiting is finished as shown and is now ready for the sliding knot.

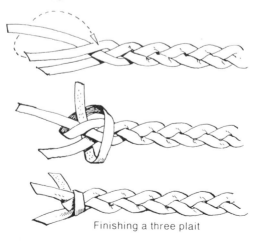

Finishing a three plait

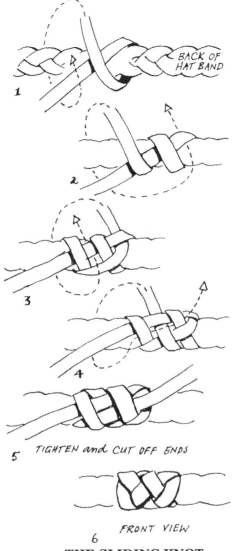

BACK OF HAT BAND

1

2

3

4

5 TIGHTEN and CUT OFF ENDS

6 FRONT VIEW

THE SLIDING KNOT
(5 part, 2 bight Turk's-head)

The sliding knot is used to keep the hat band together, one knot can be used but a pair are better. The sliding knot is a type of Turk's Head and this is an easy one to tie.

Turn the hat band inside out to begin, this puts the untidy side of the sliding knot on the inside and out of sight. Follow the sketches and when the knot has been worked tight cut off the ends and turn the band the right way round as shown in sketch 6.

The correct name for this knot is a 5 part, 2 bight Turk's-head.

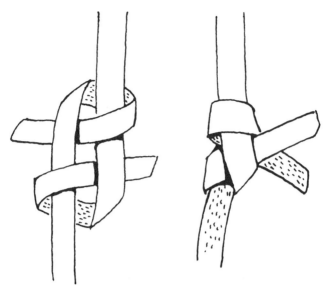

Grass bend (for tying reins)

THE GRASS BEND

The grass bend, or grass knot, is so called because it is one of the few knots that will tie together two flat blades of grass. Its main use today is to tie two straps together. The knot must be pulled tight carefully. The second sketch shows how it changes shape when tightened.

EYE SPLICE IN THE BIGHT

This is a tricky way to create a loop anywhere along the length of a piece of rope. The information came to me from a professional rigger, Graham Foster of Stratford, Queensland.

The rope is grasped firmly and twisted in opposite directions - this will cause three twisted strands to feed out as shown in the second sketch. A loop is then formed and threaded through as shown in figure 4.

Each strand is spliced into the rope in the sequence of over one strand and under one in the same way as the ordinary eye splice. The finished result is shown in figure 5.

The great knot expert Ashley did not like this knot, saying that it would damage the rope. However, he was writing in the days of natural fibre ropes and this may have had a bearing on his views; I have tied it with synthetic rope and found that it can be undone without leaving a trace on the rope.

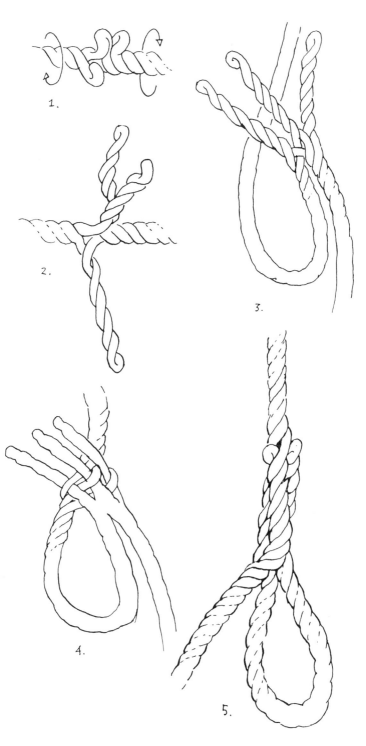

1.

2.

3.

4.

5.

TELLING A HORSE'S AGE

The horse has a front and back set of teeth. The front teeth are called the incisors and it is from these that the horse's age is judged. Behind the front teeth there is a gap (this is where the bit fits) and then right back and usually out of sight there are the molars.

Like humans, the horse first has a set of milk teeth. The foal has a complete set of front milk teeth at 8 months. By 2 years the milk teeth are fully grown and showing signs of wear. At 3 the front permanent teeth will be seen.

The two front teeth are called the centrals, and between 3 1/2 and 4 years the permanent teeth next to those, called the middle teeth, will have grown. Between 41/2 and 5 the final front permanent teeth, the corners, will have appeared.

With all the permanent teeth in place the marks on the teeth must now be studied to judge the age. Between 5 and 6 all the teeth will show black concentric rings. At 6 the black marks on the central teeth begin to fade. At 7 the marks on the middle teeth fade and at 8 the corner ones also fade.

From here on the judging of age requires considerable skill and the sketches given here can only be regarded as a general guide. The forward sloping of the teeth increases as the horse ages - the most obvious mark of an old horse.

The little rhymes that go with the sketches may help in recalling the signs that indicate the different ages.

milk teeth fully grown

dark rings

2 Years

At the age of two
The teeth are new.

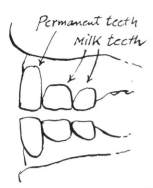

Permanent teeth
Milk teeth

As the horse ages the teeth change shape from full oval to triangular

3 Years

At the age of three
The front pair we see.

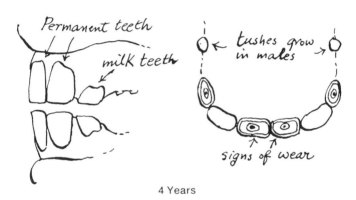

Permanent teeth

milk teeth

tushes grow in males

signs of wear

4 Years

At four there are four
And the front pair are wore.

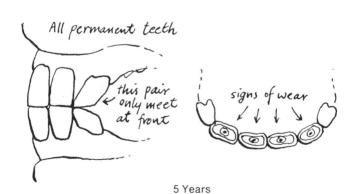

All permanent teeth

this pair only meet at front

signs of wear

5 Years

Corner teeth don't meet at five
But permanent teeth have all arrived.

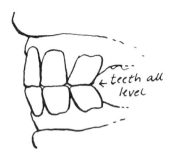

6 Years

Dark marks at six
No gaps to fix.

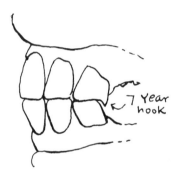

7 Years

The seven year hook will now appear,
And dark marks are no longer clear.

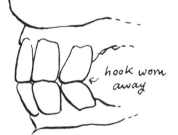

8 Years

When the age is eight
Dark lines show the date.

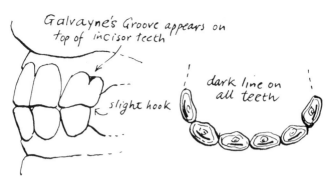

9 Years

Galvayne's Groove, small hook, dark lines,
All show that the age is nine.

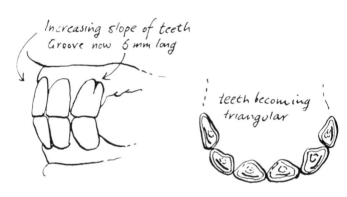

10 Years

Teeth triangular and sloping, then
The groove is growing, now he's ten.

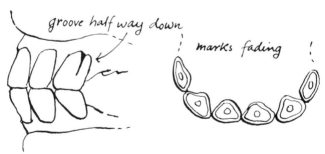

15 Years

Groove half way, dark marks not seen,
The age must be about fifteen.

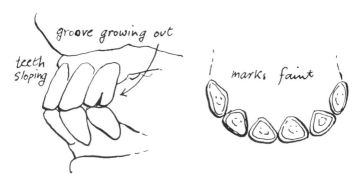

The groove grows out, he's over twenty,
And his teeth are sloping plenty.

HARNESS

Harness making is a highly-skilled craft and outside the scope of the untrained, but every bushman and farmer could repair harness in the days when all farm work and transport was by horsepower.

The horse as a working animal all but disappeared from the scene after the Second World War and it is only recently that a small but growing interest in the subject has again emerged. People who have obtained a few acres and a horse often express a desire to use the animal on the property but do not know what to do about the problem of harness.

New harness is almost unobtainable, and in any case it is very expensive if it can be found. Sometimes useable items of harness are found on old farms, but the problem then arises of identifying them and the sketches included here may help.

Although at first glance each piece of equipment may appear to differ from the one in the next drawing, a closer look will show that the difference is superficial and that the harness can be divided into a standard number of pieces each with its own purpose.

The horse pulls from its shoulders, and two things are needed to allow it to do this properly. First there is a collar which is padded to spread the pressure. The horse cannot pull from the actual collar because it has to be made flexible, and if a direct pull was put on it would distort out of shape and would put pressure on the horse's windpipe.

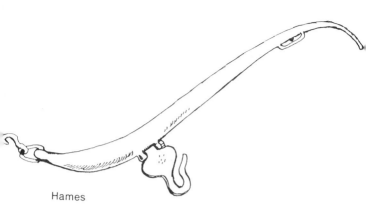

Hames

The pull is taken by two rigid pieces called hames. These sit one on each side of the collar and towards the front. At the bottom they have either a ring or a hook and either a chain or a strap is attached to this to take the pull. Towards their top they have a ring to take the reins.

Hames are often found on old farms, and because they are decorative frequently end up hanging on people's walls. The one in my sketch was picked up in the bush. This one has a hook to take the chain while in the drawing of the dray harness you will see it has a ring. There are many such small differences in each piece of harness discovered but they become less confusing once the broad purpose of each item is understood.

Working back from the collar and hames we come to the saddle, sometimes called the ridge pad. Like a riding saddle, this is also padded and its purpose is to support the weight of the shafts of the cart and also some of the weight of the load. Of course, if the cart and its load were perfectly balanced and the road was absolutely flat there would be no weight, but in practice there is.

Sometimes in a two-wheeled vehicle the weight can get too far back and tend to lift the shafts upwards and the bellyband helps to prevent the whole harness from lifting off the horse. In normal use it hangs loose as in the sketches. Underneath it will usually be a girth strap holding the saddle firmly in place, and this one has to be tight.

Around the horse's back legs will be seen a breeching strap. This is needed when the horse has to move the cart backwards. It is also needed to hold the cart in place when going down hills, and a crupper under the tail also helps keep the harness in place on hills.

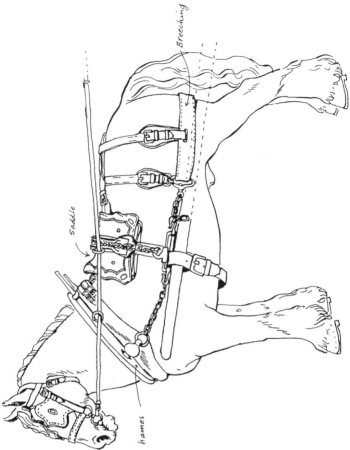

Dray Harness

Above is an example of old style dray harness, note how much more robust all the components are when compared to the harness shown on the next pages.

Harness components come in a wide variety of styles, but once their fundamental uses have been understood it is possible to reconstruct useable harness from bits and pieces picked up in a variety of places.

For pulling farm implements without shafts the harness is much simpler as the saddle and breeching are not needed. The pull is direct from the collar and hames.

The person who would like to use horsepower on his land but cannot find either old or new harness is facing a problem, as the making of this type of harness depends on a high degree of skill in the art of saddlery. Harness in Australia became specialised because it was made by specialists.

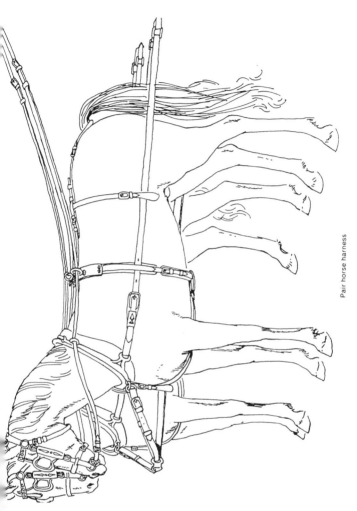

Pair Horse Harness

The detailed studies of harness given here were copied from two catalogues of 1911, and represent only a few of the many styles available at that time. There is no standard design for harness, no single 'true' pattern any more than there is one single standard motor car. However, the basic functions remain the same whatever variations of design occur.

In this harness for a pair you will note that the breeching is not needed, for when the horses have to reverse the pull comes from the straps at the front of the centre pole.

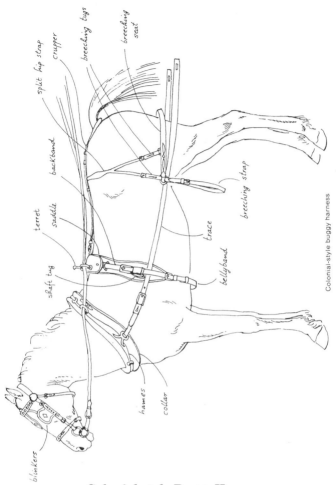

Colonial-style buggy harness

Labels on image: split hip strap, crupper, breeching tugs, breeching seat, backband, terret, saddle, shaft tug, blinkers, hames, collar, trace, bellyband, breeching strap

Colonial-style Buggy Harness

Compare this to the dray harness of the same period and you see how much lighter and more graceful this harness is.

Because many people who are interested in self-sufficiency today would like to use horses as a source of power I would like to present some ideas in harness which although not Australian are truly handmade and which do not rely on any skill to construct.

Chinese Harness

The following few drawings have been prepared from sketches and photographs that I took in China and are typical of those found in the north and central areas. The first interesting point is that although the style and materials used differ widely from ours yet the principles remain the same.

There is a collar to protect the neck and hames go against this to take the strain of the load. There is a band that goes over the back with padding for a saddle and another band around the belly.

The drawings of collar and harness were made at Dazhai, a village in the province of Shansi in northern China, situated 1000 metres above sea level in the Taihang Mountains.

China is a nation of self-sufficiency and this little mountain village in the shadow of Tiger Head Hill became famous throughout the country as the supreme example of self sufficiency at its highest level. Almost every metre of cultivated soil had been cleared from what was, only a few years before, a barren, moon-like landscape of deep, rock-strewn ravines.

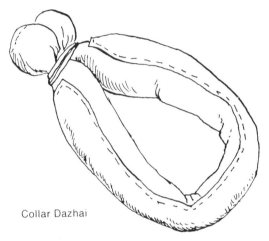

Collar Dazhai

These bits of harness are not presented as examples of skilled work; they are in fact robust but rough. The villagers' skill was in the creation of land that would grow crops in the very place where their parents and grandparents had died of starvation.

The collar illustrated above was simply made. A long tube was made of cotton, seemingly two or three layers were used to give it some strength, and this was stuffed with straw and sewn up at each end. The ends were then tied together at the top.

Leather is not such a common commodity as it is in our country, because the Chinese are not great meat eaters, and so it is used sparingly. In this case a layer was sewn on to the outside of the collar to prevent damage to the cotton - the leather was quite thin and may have been goat.

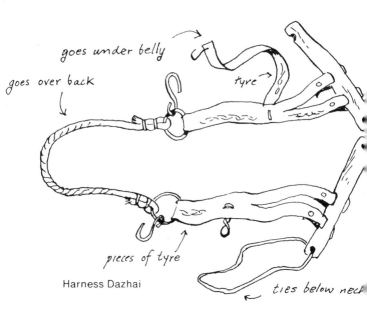

goes under belly

goes over back

tyre →

pieces of tyre

ties below neck

Harness Dazhai

I sketched this early in the morning before the horses and donkeys had been taken out to the fields. Near the collar the main piece of the harness was laid out on the ground as shown in the sketch above.

The hames were simply made out of pieces of natural timber, not sawn to shape. They went round the front of the collar and tied below the neck. The straps that took the weight of the load were attached to the hames, and in this case were made of used rubber from what looked like motorbike tyres, though it was probably rubber from the tyres of the small carts used in the area.

The band that went under the belly tied with a wire hook and was also of rubber. A rope went over the back and, to avoid hurting the horse, padding was put under it where it touched the back. Most harness was made entirely with rope though sometimes webbing was used or, as in this case, old tyres.

The next sketches show other varieties of harness, all simply constructed from readily available materials.

Drawing 1 is of the harness on a mule pulling a cart; this was near the Great Wall of China, north of Beijing. Although it may look different, if you compare it with the 1911 drawing of the dray harness it will be seen to consist of the same basic components. The collar and hames are as described earlier, the saddle made up from two simple curved pieces of timber fixed to two cross pieces.

①

Below this is a square of leather and under that the padding. As in a riding saddle there is a gap in the padding above the backbone.

A strap made of material, perhaps canvas, goes across the saddle and down to the shafts of the cart. The breeching also joins the shaft at the same point, and though made of webbing is substantially of the same shape as that used in our harness. The hames are also attached to the shafts, this time by three or four turns of rope around them. The belly-band hangs down loosely.

Sketch 2 shows a donkey and a horse near Beijing, such mixed teams are quite common. Note the use of wooden toggles on the donkey harness to attach the ropes from the hames, this saves having to tie knots and makes for easier harnessing. There are no reins, the driver relied on voice and a flick of the whip to direct his team.

(3)

Sketch 3 is of a pair near Chengchow on the Yellow River. In the central areas the collars are a slightly different pattern, wider at the top. The saddle is a roll of cotton with straw padding inside. One of the team has a muzzle, presumably to stop it nibbling the crop when it is being used in the fields.

Just as I finished writing about Chinese harness I had a visit from the son of a friend saying that he had a horse that he wanted to use on his farm but that he could not find any suitable harness. Building a collar on the British pattern was out of the question because he did not have the tools or the skill.

I showed him these sketches and he went off and made a cloth collar and wooden hames as described here, and said that they worked well.

Collar Making

For those interested in making an Australian style horse collar there are full instructions given in *Bushcraft 7.*

MAKING A HORSE RUG

A few years ago we decided to make a horse rug using an old one as a pattern. This worked quite well and lasted for many years.

The best material from which to make a rug is heavy, waterproof, flax canvas. We didn't have any of this, but what we did have was the old canvas roof from the Land Rover, and this was just big enough to make a rug. We used the existing rug for a pattern, folded our section of canvas, and marked it out as shown on the next page.

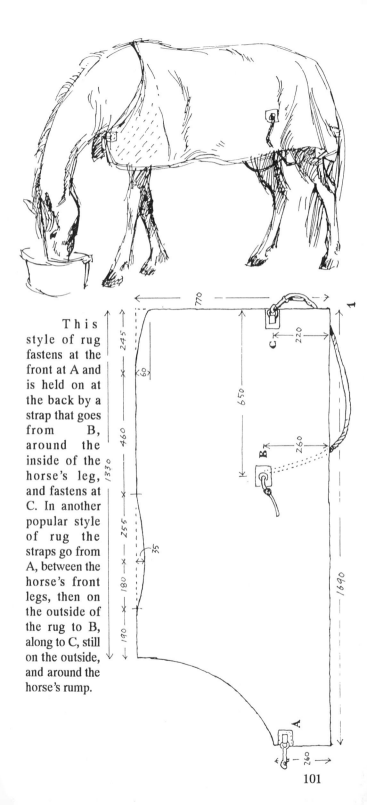

This style of rug fastens at the front at A and is held on at the back by a strap that goes from B, around the inside of the horse's leg, and fastens at C. In another popular style of rug the straps go from A, between the horse's front legs, then on the outside of the rug to B, along to C, still on the outside, and around the horse's rump.

101

We cut out the shape of the rug and tried it on the mare. We had not shaped the line of the back and the rug hung very poorly. Now we pinched up the material along the backbone and marked the proper shape. Rather than cut the material at this point we turned the rug inside out, as shown in the sketch below, and stitched up the material.

These two folded flaps of material were not visible in the finished rug, were no trouble to the mare, and saved having to cut the material at this vital point of strain. We made the rug up as shown but the mare lay down during the night and in the morning the rug had come off her, the front fastening torn away from the material.

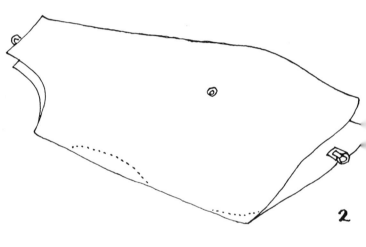

2

Obviously this point takes a considerable amount of strain when the horse gets up, or perhaps when she rolls on her side, and we noticed that our old rug had been reinforced at this point so we had to do the same.

Another piece of material was sewn on inside with plenty of stitching, as shown in 3, a piece of leather 100 mm x 70 mm sewn on to this and a piece of strap with the fastener riveted on to it with copper rivets.

It is a bad mistake to do any work with plated bifurcated rivets; eventually the plating comes off and the rivet rusts and rots through the leather. I won't use this type of rivet for any sort of work now; the copper rivets and roves are easy to attach, look better, and last longer. I used a snap fastener for fastening the front, but an ordinary buckle will also do the job.

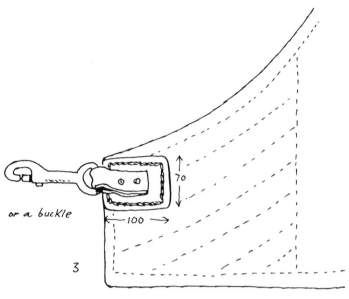

Next a piece of leather was sewn on to the centre, as shown in B in figure 1 and in detail in the sketch below. An eyelet was put into this and a piece of rope passed through and knotted. This rope passed on the inside of the horse's leg, and the position of the knot could be changed to suit different horses.

Another way to handle this problem of adjustment is to use a leather strap and attach a buckle to the piece of leather. A slot is then cut through the rug and the strap is passed through and attached to the buckle.

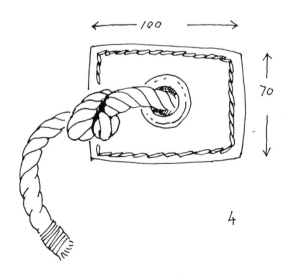

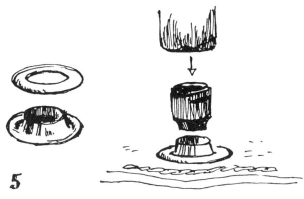

5

For my purposes the eyelet provided the simplest and easiest method. I used brass sail eyelets - we always keep a few and they come in handy for a variety of jobs. They come in two pieces as shown in 5.

To spread the eyelet and clinch it over I use the little piece of metal shown in the sketch. As I remember, it comes off the front axle of a bicycle, and is just the right size for the job. A couple of smart taps with the hammer and the eyelet is firmly in place.

If you have an engineer's hammer with a ball on it this can be used as a spreading tool. Place the ball on the eyelet and then hit the face of the hammer with another hammer, this is more accurate than trying to hit the eyelet directly with the ball.

The back piece of leather was now sewn on as shown in 6. I put it on in the simplest way as sketched on the left. It would have been neater to have passed the ends through a slot in the leather and fasten them as shown in the right-hand sketch.

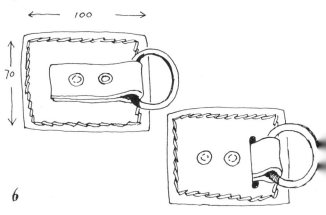

6

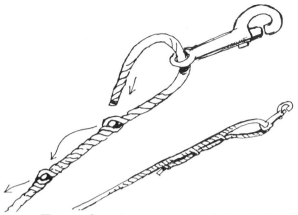

The rope from the centre was attached to the ring with another snap fastener on the rope that came from the centre eyelet. I fixed this fastener on with the simple splice shown.

A fisherman showed me this method years ago, it is simple and yet strong and the rope can be undone whenever required. It would have been neater to have used a proper eye splice, but we were in sandy country and our experience was that the fasteners do not last very long, so it is best to attach them so that they can be easily renewed.

In a cold climate a blanket would also be sewn inside the rug but being in the tropics we did not feel this was necessary. However, one old horseman suggested that we should make the canvas waterproof with a mixture of paraffin wax, melted and blended with kerosene.

We did this but found that it was not very easy to apply. However it did improved the water resistance of the material and lasted for the life of the rug.

We also applied a good coating of leather dressing to the leather pieces as we have discovered over the years that it is easier to apply leather dressing than to be forever replacing leather that has cracked and dried out.

HOBBLES

In *Australian Traditional Bush Crafts* I showed a type of hobble strap made up on the stations and fastened with a buckle. The pair shown on the next page were makeshift ones that could be knocked up along the track.

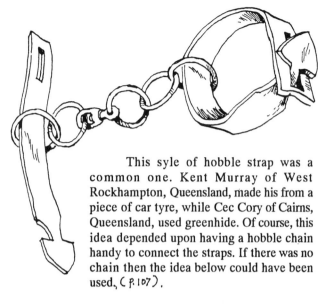

This syle of hobble strap was a common one. Kent Murray of West Rockhampton, Queensland, made his from a piece of car tyre, while Cec Cory of Cairns, Queensland, used greenhide. Of course, this idea depended upon having a hobble chain handy to connect the straps. If there was no chain then the idea below could have been used. (p.107).

SWAG STRAP INTO HOBBLES

Although swagmen are a thing of the past the swag still lives on among Australian stockmen. The stockman always travels with his bedding and clothes in a roll, wrapped around with a swag cover, and held together with a couple of straps.

When camping in the open, which he may do for most of the year, the swag cover goes right around him. This cover is usually just a rectangle of waterproof canvas, but some stockmen prefer to have them specially made.

My stockmen friends know all sorts of tricks. Les Callope then working on Dagworth Station, Queensland, showed me this next simple but clever trick of turning a strap inside out.

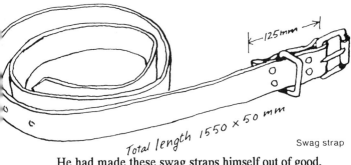

Total length 1550 × 50 mm

Swag strap

He had made these swag straps himself out of good, solid leather - the best for the job is bridle or light harness leather. The buckle and the keeper below it were held in place with four copper rivets. Nickel-plated rivets would eventually rust and rot the leather. The keeper was made by taking a buckle the same size as that used on the strap and removing the tongue.

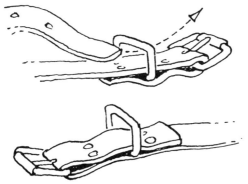

To turn the belt inside out the end of it was passed through the keeper as shown. When the whole of the strap was pulled through the keeper ended up on the wrong side of the strap! This is logical, but it still surprises me.

He then formed the strap into a figure eight as shown. He said that he used this when he wanted to tie up a bullock and didn't have anything else handy. It could also serve as makeshift hobbles.

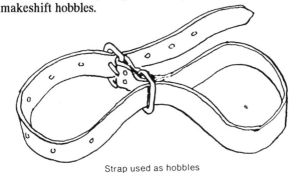

Strap used as hobbles

SPLIT BAGS

Mrs Lola O'Brien of Gordonvale, Queensland, reminded me of the simplest of all saddle bags, the split bag. To make this was the work of only a few minutes. A hessian bag, usually an old feed bag or corn sack was simply sewn up along its opening and a slit was made in it half way down.

This turned it into a pair of pockets. If it was to be used a lot then the cut edges would be turned over and hemmed so that the threads did not come loose.

This could then be thrown over the shoulder so that it formed a container with a back and front pocket, or it could be thrown over a saddle in place of a pack saddle. By putting it over a saddle the horse would not get a sore back.

In the early 1960s I went bush with Bob Keddy and Billy Ahbu of Mount Carbine, Queensland, and the sketch is from a photo that I took at the time showing the split bag thrown over the saddle.

Split Bag On A Ridden Horse

When a split bag is carried on a ridden horse it is usually thrown across the withers or tied on behind the saddle.

Mrs Price of Campsie, New South Wales, told me of this idea where the split bag does not have to be tied on but goes on top of the saddle cloth and under the back of the saddle. The saddle holds it in place and prevents it slipping backwards.

Bag cut & folded back inside

When used in this way the opening in the bag is made larger than the previous version, as shown in this sketch. This means that the pockets can be reached without removing the saddle.

This idea also does away with having to hem the cut edges as they are tucked inside the pockets out of the way.

Simple Pack Saddle Bags

Mrs Lola O'Brien sent me a description of these bags with a photo showing their packhorses being loaded for the climb up Mount Spurgeon in north Queensland.

Saddle bags made by a professional saddler were very expensive so the pioneers looked around for a home-made solution. Fresh untanned bullock hide was available whenever a beast was killed for the table, and so this was used.

The light pine box that kerosene tins came in was used as the foundation for the bags. The rawhide was cut so that it wrapped completely round the box, including enough for a flap, and was left to dry and harden into shape. Some temporary tacks would have been used to hold it in place as the leather would shrink as it dried.

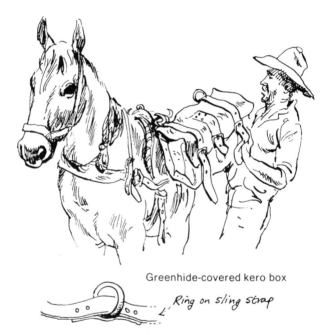

Greenhide-covered kero box

Ring on sling strap

When it was dry the box was removed and the ends of the greenhide riveted together with copper rivets. The box was then replaced. Sling straps went around the bag with a ring fixed as shown and this ring fixed the bag to the pack saddle.

An extra strap in the centre also held the flap down. Lola said that the flimsy pine boxes would break up in time, but by then the bags would have become permanently moulded into shape.

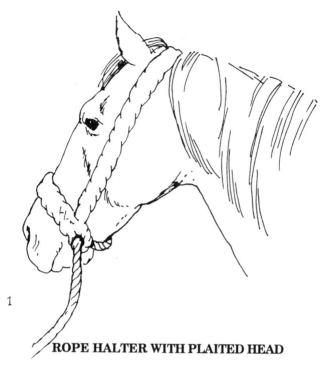

1

ROPE HALTER WITH PLAITED HEAD

I noted this halter near Myola, north Queensland. Commercially made ones of the same design are common, but they have much finer plaiting, up to twelve strands, and use cotton rope.

The one that I am describing here was made from sisal rope of between 45 mm and 55 mm circumference. The heavier rope looks better, but the thinner rope is strong enough if the heavier material is not available. Sisal rope is now hard to get, but synthetic rope can be used if it is not too slippery.

A rope of around 4 metres is used, and the three strands of the rope unravelled back for a distance of 1.630 m. Each of these three strands is then halved, so that six strands are formed, as shown below.

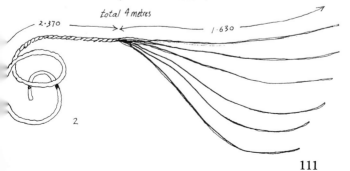

total 4 metres

2·370   1·630

2

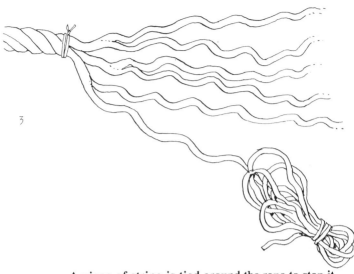

3

A piece of string is tied around the rope to stop it unravelling any further (this can be done before the strands are unravelled). For ease in plaiting the ends of the strands can be rolled up and held with a rubber band as shown in 3.

Now the six strands are spread out flat, and held in that position with a couple of sticks or pencils which can be tied together or held with rubber bands as shown.

Now we begin the plaiting, which is called a six-strand French sennit, I believe that the French call it an English sennit. It is simple to do, and only two actions are needed. First the left hand outside strand is brought over one and under one as shown in 4.

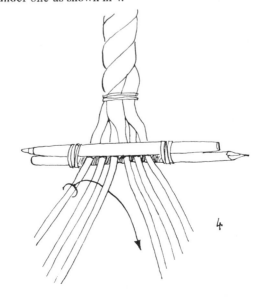

4

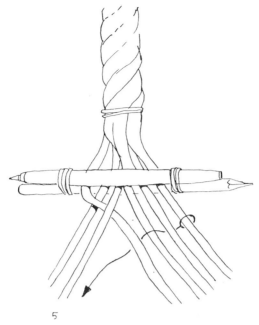

5

We now have four strands in one hand and two in the other. Now the outside right strand is brought under one, over one, under one, as shown in 5, above.

This brings us back to the beginning, with three strands in each hand, and the first action is then repeated, as in 6, and so on.

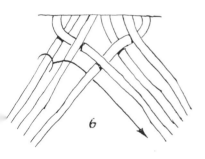

6

The final plait will look something like 7. Plaiting continues for 820 mm.

7

8

Now each pair of strands are twisted together for about 100 mm in the direction shown in 8.

These three strands are then twisted together in the opposite direction as in 9, thus re-forming the rope back into its original shape.

This is now turned around to form a loop large enough to take the rope later. The newly-formed section is now split back into six strands and each strand threaded back as indicated in 10.

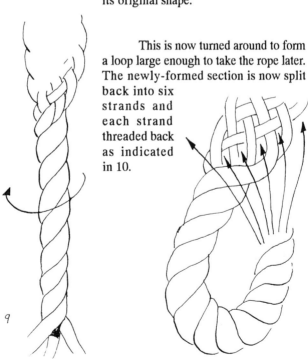

9

10

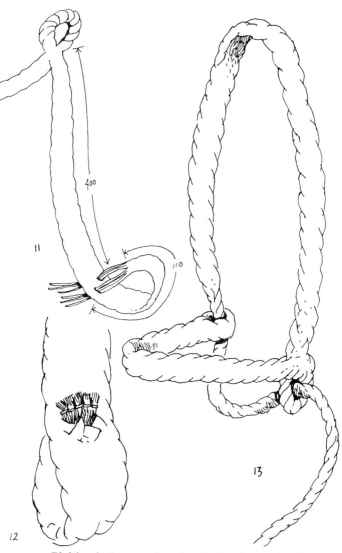

Plaiting is then continued as before for another 510 mm. A second loop is now formed by dividing the strands into two groups and passing them through the plaited section 110 mm from the end as shown in 11.

The ends are then tightly sewn as shown in 12 and the surplus cut off to complete the halter. An even neater way to finish off would be to pass each strand through individually and plait it back into the material, but this is not really necessary.

The end of the rope is then threaded through loops as shown in 13 and the halter is complete.

ROPE BRIDLES

This must be the most simple rope bridle of all and is the one my wife often used when bringing the horses home. The rope is simply doubled and folded over itself as shown and the bridle is complete. A minimum of 5 metres of rope is needed for this and the following method.

Because this bridle is made in such a loose manner it can only be used with horses that are quiet and trained to neck rein.

The next method takes the previous system a step further. The same initial crossing is made, and then a loop from the rein end is pulled through as in figure 2 to make the nose band.

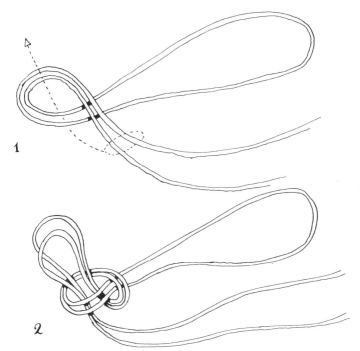

It will be seen that as the reins are pulled so the nose loop is made tight, and because of this only thick, soft rope should be used - to avoid any chance of it jamming and not releasing the pressure when the reins are relaxed.

The major drawback to both the above methods is that the rope tends to slip down the horse's neck if it throws its head about.

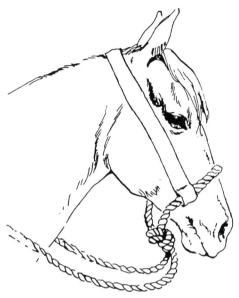

This next method is much more satisfactory, and was sketched at the cutting competitions at Mareeba in 1974. John Bashem used this bridle on the mare that he rode in the competition.

The head band is made from a piece of cotton webbing sewn on to a rope as shown. This rope is knotted and the bridle is complete.

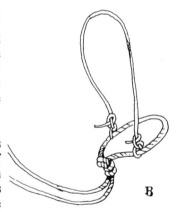

B

A similar type of bridle can be constructed with two pieces of rope as shown in figure B.

Some other styles of rope bridles are shown in *Bushcraft 1,* and the most popular of all, based on the Fiador knot, may be found in *Bushcraft 5.*

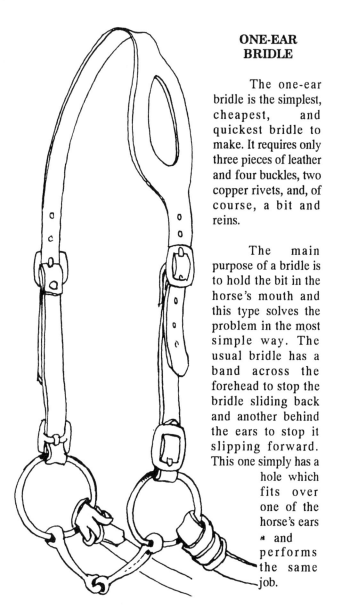

ONE-EAR BRIDLE

The one-ear bridle is the simplest, cheapest, and quickest bridle to make. It requires only three pieces of leather and four buckles, two copper rivets, and, of course, a bit and reins.

The main purpose of a bridle is to hold the bit in the horse's mouth and this type solves the problem in the most simple way. The usual bridle has a band across the forehead to stop the bridle sliding back and another behind the ears to stop it slipping forward. This one simply has a hole which fits over one of the horse's ears and performs the same job.

By having only one hole it will fit all sizes of horses - if there were two holes then the horse would have to have its ears that certain distance apart.

CHEEK PIECES FOR BRIDLES

The sketch above show a cheek piece for a stallion bridle, and are drawn from a saddler's catalogue of 1911. A bridle fitted out in this way is very decorative, especially when new and with the colours bright. I made one some years ago, but after twelve months constant use and a few applications of saddle dressing the colours had almost gone.

It would probably be better to make a second cheek piece of ordinary strap and only use the fancy one when required.

The back of the cheek piece is made from bridle leather, and the decorations from any thin, coloured, leather scraps that come to hand. This one had an outer area of thin calf with padding under it.

(There is more information about this and other bridles in *Bushcraft 2.*)

BROKEN REINS

The late Harry Dawkins, one of my old friends, once took off his belt and chopped it up in order to show me this simple way of repairing broken reins. After this dramatic demonstration he put the belt back around his trousers with never a second thought.

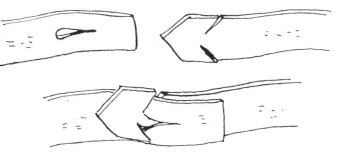

Repairing broken reins

This is intended as a temporary makeshift to get the rider home safely and not as a permanent method of joining reins.

MENDING REINS

Here is another method of mending reins. It looks neater than the previous method but takes longer. As mentioned above these repairs are only intended to get the rider home where the leather should be replaced at once.

This idea came from Ken Lomman of Naracoorte, South Australia, and George Leighfield of Glenroy, Victoria.

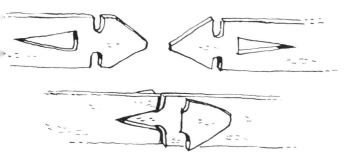

Mending reins

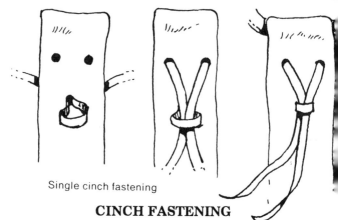

Single cinch fastening

CINCH FASTENING

This fastening is usually used to fasten a cinch to a saddle but it can be used to fasten any strap to a ring or buckle. The single one is the most common and is quick and easy to tie. A saddle that came into our shop for repairs had a double fastening which would be very useful when only lighter quality lace is on hand to fasten the strap.

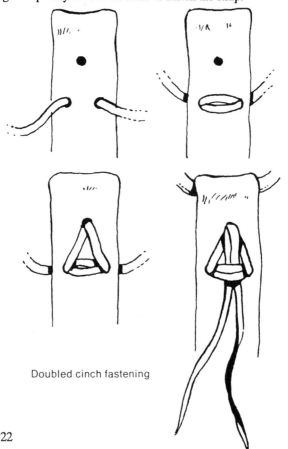

Doubled cinch fastening

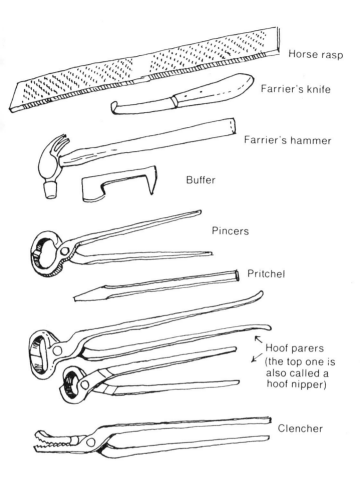

Horse rasp

Farrier's knife

Farrier's hammer

Buffer

Pincers

Pritchel

Hoof parers
(the top one is
also called a
hoof nipper)

Clencher

TOOLS FOR HORSE SHOEING

Many new horse owners do not realise that whether or not they do a lot of riding their horse must have its shoes removed at regular intervals. They think that once on the shoe can stay there till it wears out.

This is not so, the hoof grows all the time and can grow right around the shoe if it is not removed. There is no set time for removing the shoes but generally they need to come off every six weeks.

Every horse owner should have some basic tools even if he or she does not do his own shoeing. At the very least he or she should have a farrier's knife to keep the sole of the hoof clean. It is also an advantage to be able to remove the shoes. Sometimes a shoe will become loose and it should then be removed at once.

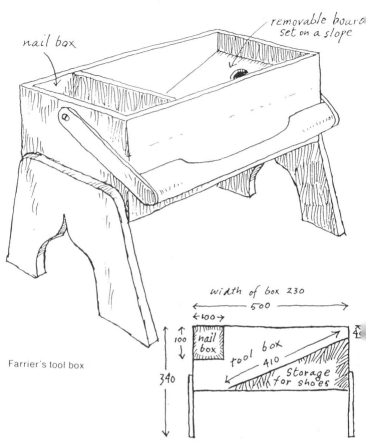

nail box

removable board
set on a slope

Farrier's tool box

width of box 230

500

←100→

nail box

tool box
410

Storage
for shoes

100

340

FARRIER'S BOX

If you have ever shod a horse you will know that it is
bad enough to be holding up half an animal without the
added frustration of fumbling around on the ground for tools.
The farrier's box brings the tools and nails up to a height
where they can be reached without having to let go the
horse's hoof.

I have seen a number of variations of these boxes and
this seems to be the most convenient. The height of the box
from the ground can be altered to suit. The tools lie on a
sloping board with their handles up so that they can be easily
grasped. Items not needed during the shoeing are stored
below the sloping board.

The nails are in a handy position and away from the
tools while the handle drops out of the way. Any small
packing case could be modified in some way to make a tool
box like this (though these days wooden boxes are rare).

Some Ideas

Here are a few useful ideas drawn from a variety of sources. The bridge illustrated below is a good example of the use of fencing wire, and another variation on this style of bridge may be found in *Bushcraft 4* page 152.

BUSH BRIDGE

This description of a bush bridge was sent to me by historian Glenville Pike who found it in a copy of *The Queenslander* of 1895. It was in an article titled *Some Northern Stations* by 'Basalt'. This is what Basalt had to say:

"On reaching the river (on Southwick Station) I beheld a dangerous looking bridge, but although it would be a trifle risky for any but a sober man to negotiate I saw on closer examination that it was a bridge that many a selector or country resident would appreciate, so sitting down I penned the following description of what I would call a cheap, reliable, easily constructed wire suspension bridge.

"The design is simplicity itself and requires no engineering beyond what a smart stockman or selector is capable of mastering. On the near bank two strong posts are planted and well secured. At the back of the posts on the side away from the water is placed a horizontal post well lashed to the uprights.

"Through this post are bored eight equidistant holes and through these holes are secured the ends of eight separate pieces of strong, plain galvanised wire, each piece being of sufficient length to span the stream with some to spare.

"Tough boards are laid on and lashed to these wires a foot or so apart form the footway. At each end of the steps a hole is bored large enough to put the wire through.

"Placing the outside wires through these holes is sufficient for the remaining six to be placed under and over the steps as the case may be. On the other bank similar posts and cross-bar are erected and the wire secured in the same manner as before, leaving the bridge suspended from bank to bank with a slight dip in the middle.

"In this state, unless one is a tight-rope walker, it would be next to impossible to cross. The missing link is a single wire on each side, secured to the perpendicular posts, about 7' 6" (2.2 metres) above the foundation wires and joined every yard or so with the bridge by means of short pieces of wire.

"If left at this state the bridge would oscillate rapidly but wire guys to the bank on either side steady it. After a little practice a man finds it no trouble to negotiate with his arms full."

I have based my sketches on this description, the one below shows a detail of construction.

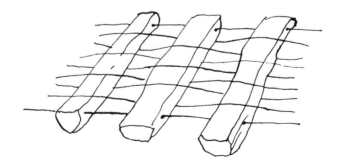

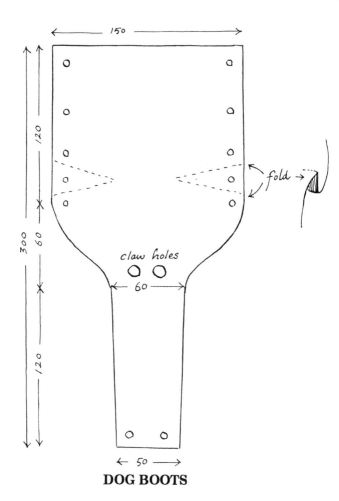

DOG BOOTS

Dog boots are needed if a dog has a damaged pad or is working in very harsh country. They are made from suede or soft leather and are tied on with leather lace.

The average dog is not at all helpful when you are trying to work out a boot pattern so I would suggest that you first cut out a paper pattern using these measurements as a guide, try this on the dog, and make your adjustments on the paper rather than risk ruining the leather.

To fit the boot the dog's front two claws go through the holes and the thin flap of leather folds up the front of its leg and is laced on. The back flap then ties around the foot and laces at the front as shown.

Another style of dog boot may be found in *Bushcraft* 7 page 130, one that is intended for slightly heavier leather.

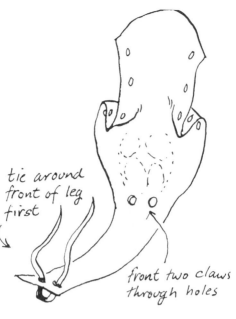

tie around front of leg first

front two claws through holes

Each dog has a different size foot, and so the pattern given here can only be used as a guide. I made it for our blue cattle dog who was just a little smaller than a Labrador.

Try out a pattern cut from a piece of paper first before cutting the leather.

MEN'S BRACES

Around the turn of the century men's braces were solid, down-to-earth articles, not the effete objects seen today. They were made by saddlers, and used the same techniques as found in harness making.

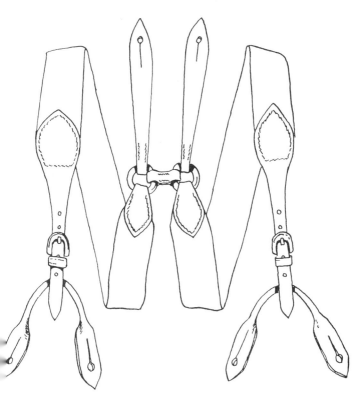

These two examples came from a saddler's catalogue published in 1911. The first one had 38mm (1 1/2") webbing straps with brass rings at the back and buckles at the front. The centre section of the straps that go from the front trousers buttons was rolled and sewn into a circular shape.

The second example, on the next page, was made of all leather, brass rings and buckles. Notice the formidable three-tongue buckles. I don't think that these are obtainable anywhere today, but a two tongue buckle known as a gear buckle is still being made.

The straps for these braces were 38 mm wide, but similar types were made up to 60 mm wide. The webbing-strapped braces sold for 8 cents a pair, the all leather ones were 9 cents.

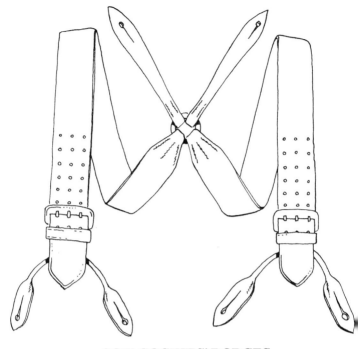

COW COCKIES' DODGES

K. McAuliffe of Katanning, Western Australia, wrote to remind me of some of the ideas used by small farmers in the old days, and some which are still being used today.

The first sketch is of a cow bail. The cow put its head through the space to eat the food and the stick was moved and fixed with a bolt through the hole so that it could not withdraw its head.

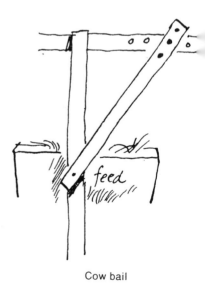

Cow bail

The sticks did not press against the neck, but were just adjusted so that the gap prevented the horns being pulled through the space.

We used a similar idea in southern Victoria, but the pivoting stick was longer and began nearer the floor. We would also have a metal ring and rope attached to the wall and the rope would be tied to the cow's lower leg on the side on which it was being milked to stop it from kicking over the bucket.

(Another type of cow bail is illustrated in *Bushcraft* 7 page 96.)

Eye Shade for Bulls

Bull blindfold

The second sketch is of something that I have not seen. It was used on savage bulls that made a habit of charging people.

A piece of tin with two holes in it was placed over the bull's horns and fastened around its neck with a strap. This did not interfere with its feeding but prevented it from seeing straight ahead.

Fence Saver

The third sketch is of an idea that was common in Victoria. Once a cow got into the habit of pushing its head through a fence to feed on the other side it was impossible to stop it, and broken fences were the result. To save the fencing the habitual fence breaker was fitted with a forked branch around its neck. This must have been a nuisance to the animal but at least it stopped it breaking fences.

Fencebreaker's fork

That Old Forked Stick

The cocky farmer had a great love for the forked stick and used it to make all sorts of things. In 1978 I sketched this cattle feeder based on a pair of forked sticks fixed firmly in the ground. The ends had been closed off and the grid of wire covered the sides. Hay could be forked into the top and the animals could feed without trampling and soiling their dinner.

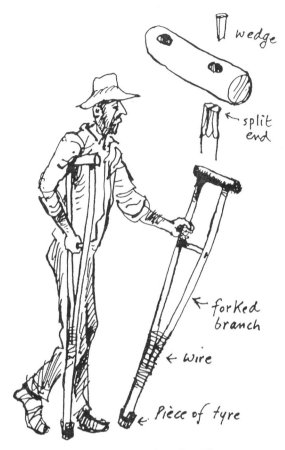

wedge

← split end

← forKed branch

← wire

← Piece of tyre

BUSH CRUTCHES

Mr V. Walker of Deniliquin, New South Wales, gave me some details of home-made crutches. I made a similar pair for myself some years ago when my mare kicked me in the leg in a burst of high spirits.

A sapling is split down its length and wire bound round the bottom of the split to stop it going the whole length of the stick. The arm rest and cross piece also are made from round pieces of bush timber and are attached as shown in the smaller sketch, by pushing them through a hole and then holding them tightly with a timber wedge.

This same method can also be used when making furniture out of bush timber.

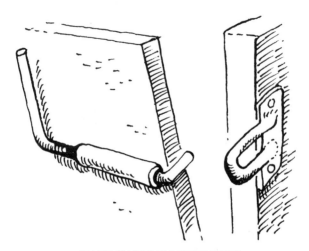

TAILGATE FASTENING

I did this sketch of a home-made tailgate fastening on a horse float at the Mareeba Rodeo some years ago. There are a lot of troublesome fasteners on horse floats and this seemed to be a very good idea.

As can be seen from the sketches it will only work with a gate that sits against the sides of the trailer, not one that slips in between the sides. The short end of the catch cannot be any longer than the width of the tailgate.

When fully fastened, as shown on the next page, the catch should be applying some pressure to the loop in the catch, and it is this that stops it rattling when the float is being towed.

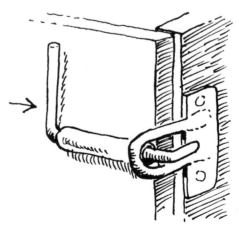

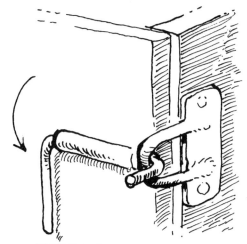

FENCING WIRE CHAIN

Some old-timers used to be able to do just about anything with a length of fencing wire. Carl Bailey, who was in his seventies when I did this sketch in 1978, made this chain out of fencing wire while working in Western Australia around 1922.

Carl was an old friend of mine and could not see anything clever about it - it was the normal thing to do in those days. He was still using some of this chain forty years after he had made it and I found it to be very strong.

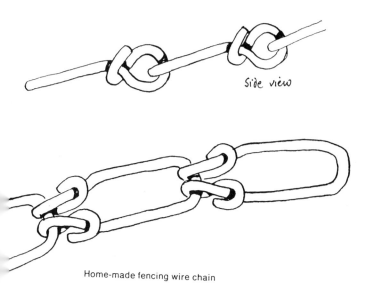

Side view

Home-made fencing wire chain

MOBILE WORK BENCH

Being able to take both the tools and the work bench right to the job would have saved the farmer some work. Most farmers had wheels from various implements around the place and some constructed variations of the idea in my sketch. Ken Lomman of Naracoorte, South Australia, and George Leighfield of Glenroy, Victoria, sent this idea.

BAG LIFTER

This idea was in an old farmer's handbook given to me by Jean and John Schwartz of Mount Gambier, South Australia. It was used to take the strain out of lifting heavy grain sacks on to the back of a cart.

A fork of bush timber had a shelf attached on which the bag could be laid. A cross piece was fixed at the top of the lifter to stop it swivelling around.

The farmer grabbed the lower ends of the fork and lifted them so that the bag was tipped on to the tray of the cart, a much easier operation than a straight dead lift.

Sometimes the lifter was made with two poles.

Bag lifter

136

STUMP FORGE

Mr W. Hickmott of Guthalungra, Queensland, told me of this idea. I have not seen it in action and so cannot comment on how effective it would be.

He said that it was used to gain enough heat to dress crowbars, pick heads, or rock drills. (Dressing consists of bringing the tool to red heat and then hammering, sharpening and pointing it.)

A dry, hollow stump was selected and a hole chopped in the bottom facing the prevailing wind. A windy day was hoped for and a fire was lit inside the stump.

The updraught created intense heat and according to Mr Hickmott 'a ten knot wind will melt a crowbar in about 15 minutes'. Obviously the efficiency of this forge would be governed by the height and diameter of the hollow stump, the force of the wind, and the type of fuel used.

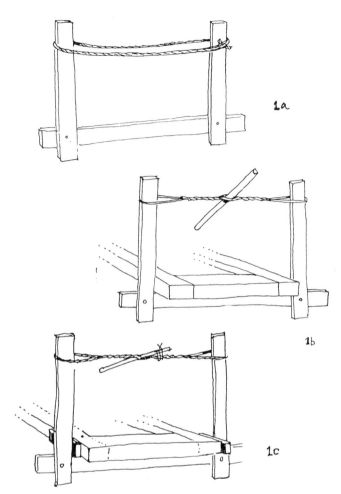

SIMPLE CLAMPS

This simple clamp is fabricated from three pieces of scrap timber and a length of rope. It is made up on the spot according to the measurements of the job being done. The two uprights are set just far enough apart to take the iob, and fixed to the bottom piece with a couple of nails simply driven through and not even bent over.

The loop of cord is dropped over as shown in la and when the job to be clamped is in position it is tightened up with a stick as in lb. When enough pressure has been applied the stick is tied back to the rope to stop it unwinding. This clamp brings pressure to bear at one point on the job rather than applying parallel pressure, and so small pieces of scrap are sometimes used on each side to avoid marking the timber, as shown in lc.

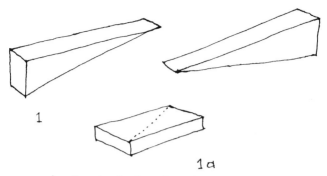

1

1a

Another simple clamp is made with a pair of wedges. These can be cut from a piece of scrap timber as in 1a, but it is more usual to pick them up on a building site from among the offcuts.

Wedges can be used for a great many clamping jobs, and have the advantage over the previous clamp of applying parallel pressure. I have used them, for instance, when putting down a floor and not having proper flooring clamps at hand.

Three or four boards can be clamped up at a time as shown in 2. The wedges are hammered together using a pair of hammers, and the pressure that is exerted is really amazing. Scrap timber is used to fill the space between the wall and the flooring. Wedges can also be used for clamping jobs on the workbench by simply nailing down pieces of scrap timber for them to work against.

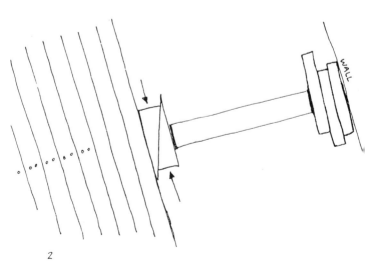

2

INDEX